Going Home

A Heart's Reflections

Shirley Ann (Damron) Stafford

WESTBOW
PRESS®
A DIVISION OF THOMAS NELSON
& ZONDERVAN

All scripture quotations, unless otherwise indicated, are taken from the King James Version of the Bible.

WestBow Press books may be ordered through booksellers or by contacting:

WestBow Press
A Division of Thomas Nelson & Zondervan
1663 Liberty Drive
Bloomington, IN 47403
www.westbowpress.com
1 (866) 928-1240

ISBN: 978-1-5127-9651-3 (sc)

Library of Congress Control Number: 2017911110

Print information available on the last page.

WestBow Press rev. date: 7/27/2017

Dedication

I dedicate this book to pastors and their wives as well as those who are in ministry. Remember that your life is one big teaching book. Keep in mind that love is the fabric that holds us all together.

To my son, Tommy, thank you for believing in me and cheering me on to accomplish this work. You are a wonderful source of inspiration to me. I will always love you, son.

To my cousin, Barbara (Rogers) Summers, I want to say a special thank you for your prayers and encouragement. You were the first one to suggest that I put my thoughts into a book. I love you as my sister, friend, and cousin.

To my family and church family, I thank you for being vital parts of my life. You've always been a source of strength to me. I hope you will be blessed by this recount of my journey in life.

To those who need to be reminded—it's the little things that truly do count.

Contents

Foreword xi

Acknowledgments xiii

Introduction xv

Going Home 1

The Bridge 3

Count the Cost 4

Build Your House upon the Rock 6

Safe Haven 7

Testing Times 9

God's Help 10

Seas of Life 12

Problem Chasers 13

Wait upon the Lord 15

Trust God 16

Next Step 18

Be Not Weary 19

Thankfulness 21

Don't Quit 22

No Quitting Time 24

Waiting 25

A Son 27

Abundant Blessings 28

Where Can I Go? 30

Living with God 31

Stand 33

Love and Compassion 34

Love Shines 36

Hero's Confidence 37

The Master's Hand 39

Knowing God 40

The Father's Love 42

Keeping It Real 43

Eagle's Wings 45

Offering Miracle 46

When You Pray 48

Mother's Heart 49

A Mother's Work 51

Full Costume 52

Quiet, Little Child 54

Unshakeable Faith 55

There May Come a Time 57

Wisdom Gained 58

I Look to You 60

Unlock the Door 61

Rocky Road 63

Secret Place 64

A Quiet Place 66

Precious Things 67

Walk within Your Will 69

The Move 70

Life Is a Painting 72

The Picture 73

Walk with Me 75

Good Thoughts 76

The Mirror 78

A Few Coins 79

My Heart Reflects 81

The Wheelbarrow 82

The Time You Gave 84

The Piano 85

What Did You Do? 87

The Revival 88

Down Life's Highway 90

The Light 91

The Homecoming Day 93

Break Down 94

Not Alone 96

The Waymaker 97

Hand of God 99

Picky Eaters 100

Cooking 102

Father's Arms 103

Carry Me 105

Childish Views 106

Tommy's Hatching Ducks 108

Whosoever 110

Before I Can See You 112

Glimpse of Heaven 113

My Glimpse of Heaven 115

Amazing Grace 116

Grace...118

Protected 119

Struggles... 121

Great Big Fat Hen...122

My Heart...124

Foreword

Shirley asked me to write an article for her book. Well, here it goes!

What a friend? What a pal? What a cousin?

I am thrilled to elaborate about our lives together. We are first cousins, not by chance but ordained by God. God protected us no matter the situations we got into.

It seems as though we were more than cousins. We were cohorts in mischief as children. We were always getting into adventures. We surfed and swam in creeks on hot summer days. Afterward, we would try to catch fish with a bucket or whatever we could find to snare them. Sometimes, we would catch minnows or crawdads.

Some of our adventures took us high in the mountains or to Omar, West Virginia. We would explore the rock formations, look inside of some of the caves, and admire the beautiful flowers in the spring. Oftentimes, we would climb the rock formations to look at the awesome views that God made and see how blue the sky really was. We would often echo our voices, which was so much fun!

I can remember vividly that one day, as we were coming down the mountains, Shirley and I heard a noise beside us. I wondered what that noise could have been.

Shirley said, "Oh, it's probably nothing," However, we both started down the hill a little faster. The faster we went, the louder the noise got, and the closer the noise was to us. Shirley looked at me, and her eyes were big as saucers. I was really scared, and so was she. We ran faster than we ever ran, but we were not fast enough to outrun whatever was following us. We decided to take a shortcut down the mountains via a path that wasn't a path anymore. There in front of us was a cliff. We knew we had to make a decision right then. Right beside us were two of the biggest black snakes we ever saw. We weren't going to let them catch us, so we jumped over the cliff.

Shirley and I didn't know whether to cry or laugh. We knew it was one of the funniest things that could happen to two little girls in the hills of Omar. We still laugh about that adventure. I thought about changing our names to Huck Finn and Tom Sawyer. Thank God that He's in the mountains as well as in the valleys of Omar.

Shirley wrote plays, and we would act out those plays in our little self-made theater with the best audience two little girls could have, our parents. We were blessed with parents who endured our poor acting and made-up costumes, and they even clapped when we were finished. (I wonder if they clapped because we were good actresses or if they wanted to get out of there.)

In school, we had a lot of classes together and some of the same friends. We also helped fight each other's battles. No one picked on cousins without help from the other. Needless to say, we had loads of fun. After school, we walked the railroad tracks. We walked the rails home, not falling off once. We were good at that! We had lots of practice.

Our childhood was great! Our families loved each other, and we still look out for each other now. We look back and laugh at the some of the things that happened. We had hard times and sad times in our lives, but you know, I wouldn't trade those times for anything. We were blessed!

Shirley is very talented. She mastered (self-taught) playing the piano and has the voice of a songbird. She is a successful artist, and she writes plays, stories, poems, and songs. She is a minister of the Lord, and the list goes on.

Thank you, Shirley, for letting me tell some of our childhood secrets.

By the way, I didn't tell everything we did. There are many more adventures. I decided to keep some of them to myself.

Love and prayers,
Barbara Summers

Acknowledgments

I want to acknowledge those who have been such a critical part of the preparation and publication of this book.

To the entire WestBow Press publishing company, thank you for your help in getting the job completed.

To my family, I want to thank you for continually offering suggestions about this book.

Introduction

I find great comfort in writing. Sometimes I escape to my quiet study to just spend time releasing my thoughts for the moment. I've written a lot of the moments in the form of poems and books. Most of them came during my time of leisure. Although I never published them, I loved doing the work.

I was influence by some of my family members to share my writings with others. It seemed like a great idea, but I wasn't sure anyone would want to read them. Either way, I promised that I would dedicate more time to releasing them. Silently, I prayed for courage.

It's taken awhile for me to do, but I'm finally on track and getting more motivated to do what comes naturally for me. Writing has always been an expression of who I am and how God made me. I hope to always reflect Him.

I've always been one who loves words, particularly the written word. I decided to combine my personal experiences with my faith walk, and you now know the reason for my writing this book. I've grown over the last forty years, and I believe that by sharing my book, I can help others.

This book is not a masterpiece, but it is my heart. I'm releasing it to the public as a real personal part of my life and journey in ministry. My goal is very simply to help others as they sift through the pages of this book.

My hope is that you find strength, courage, and wisdom as you read it. You will find my heart embedded within each page. May God bless you and inspire you to reach greater heights and deeper depths in Him. There is a wonderful home awaiting us in the eternal. We are all on a journey here on earth, but we are all headed toward home.

Going Home

When he was still a great way off, his father saw him and had
compassion, and ran and fell on his neck and kissed him.
—Luke 15:29

My husband, Tom, and I were called into ministry in 1976. We were called when we were attending a local church near our home in Plymouth, Michigan. Immediately afterward, we went back to our home state of West Virginia and began our journey in Christ's service. Our hearts were zealous for God's ministry.

Although we loved our calling as evangelists, there were times that the work became overwhelming. At other times, things happened that strengthened our resolve to keep going. One day, my husband and I were blessed as we headed out to a revival meeting. As we drove, we saw a young man hitchhiking along Route 10 in Pecks Mill, West Virginia. My husband, as he so often did, pulled over and offered the young man a ride. "Where are you headed?" he asked.

The young man replied, "I'm headed home."

My husband responded, "Home's a good place to go."

As we chatted, we informed him that we were ministers and headed to a scheduled revival. I couldn't resist asking, "Do you know the Lord?"

I could see the smile on my husband's face as he heard the question. The young man looked down and gave a sigh. "No, I don't now, but I used to."

We eagerly shared the word with him, and he accepted Christ into his heart. We listened as he shared his story with us. He had known God but walked away from Him. He got involved with the wrong crowd and became alienated from family and friends. His life was one of substance abuse and thoughts of suicide. Suddenly, he said, "Thank God. Now I'm free!"

After dropping him off at his house, he assured us that he was going back to church.

We were encouraged and thankful for the events of that day. However, a few weeks later, we heard that the young man had been killed in an accident. Hearing the news saddened our hearts, but friends assured us that he had been doing well. He had just found a job and was living for Christ.

We are all on a journey that leads us to eternity. As we walk down the highway of life, God finds us and gives us the chance to know Him. We were thankful that we had a small part in leading that young man back to the Lord. God knows all things, and His will was with us as we picked him up that day on the side of the road. It was comforting to us as we recalled the young man's last words as he got out of our car. He said, "I'm headed home."

We knew in our hearts that he was right, and we agreed. Yes, he was headed home.

"God sees a great way off those things that we can't imagine."

Shirley's Prayer
Lord, help me to face the things that are in my path today. Give me the
courage to face all my enemies with a pure heart and a kind word. Be
the shadow of my heart as I walk, and guide me in all matters of my life.
I'm confident in your power to sustain me. Thank You. Amen.

The Bridge

The bridge that aids my soul across,
Never weakens, though the winds may toss.
In myself, I could but flee,
But God's hand has stayed on me.
The perils of this passing time
May never cease, but the sun will shine.
Forever more, my soul shall see
The awesome price Christ paid for me.
Swing wide, oh bridge within my soul!
Guide my steps, and make me whole.
Keep me safe, and shield my way
As I pass over life's bridge each day.

Count the Cost

What things were gain to me, these I have counted loss for Christ.
—Philippians 1:7

I wasn't sure where I was headed when I quit my job at General Motors in Livonia, Michigan, in 1977. At the time, all we knew was that we were to surrender our lives to Christ. My husband and I had a shared vision of winning souls to Christ. We were determined that we were going to do something for God's kingdom. We began to travel in evangelism shortly after we were converted in the Full Gospel Church in Taylor, Michigan. Neither of us was prepared for the hardships we would encounter or the demands that would come with that calling. There was an endless need for travel, revivals, and visitations compounded by the struggle to keep the bills paid. We credit God for keeping us safe and protecting us from discouragement.

At first, it was difficult to get church doors opened. There were days when I wondered if our sacrifices were making any difference in the lives of others. At that time, we were evangelizing under an old-fashioned canvas tent. It was a lot of hard work. We struggled with advertising, putting the tent up, staking it down, spreading the sawdust over the front to the altar, and putting out chairs. When it rained, we had to do extra work by digging ditches to keep the rain from running into the tent. We were vigilant to loosen or tighten the tent ties when wind and storms came. After each revival, we let the canvas dry before we took it down to prevent mold.

One day, as we conducted our service under the tent, I saw something that gave me the strength to keep going. I was in the pulpit of the tent behind my organ when I happened to look out into the field. A man who sat on the hood of his pickup truck was listening to my husband's sermon. The man was drinking something that we later realized was alcohol. After the message, he got off the truck, stood up, and threw the substance down. I watched as he tucked his shirt into his trousers and came to the altar to pray. That night, he buried his knees into that sawdust and asked God into his heart. He became a new creation in Christ Jesus. That was a miracle that only God could perform. The man's actions gave me a clear message from the Lord. I couldn't help but think about what I would do if I gained the world and lost my soul.

The service that night helped my husband and me to set our priorities right and continue to do God's will. We knew the road would be paved with challenges and trials, but God would bless our commitment to Him. After that night, we were blessed to see many other services just like that one. God blessed our ministry to reach those who may never have come inside a church building.

We eventually gave up the tent. Many church doors opened up for us. Along with the doors, many more souls were added to the kingdom of God. Whenever I think of the task of ministry, God brings back a picture of the young man who came to love God that night under the old canvas tent. It was that night that I counted the cost of seeing souls won to God. What price is a soul worth?

No amount of riches could buy the essence of salvation. It was that one particular night that I realized there was a price to be paid for the work in ministry. It was under that old tent, in a weedy field on a starlit night, that God spoke to my heart to continue His work. That night, I realized it was a price that I was truly able to pay.

For what is a man profited if he gain the whole world and lose his own soul?
—Matthew 16:25

Shirley's Prayer
Lord, help me so that I don't let the miracle of your blessing be taken for granted. I can't go without reaching out and taking hold of all that you have for me. Allow me to be close to you and do all that you have for me to do. You have blessed me so much. Every blessing I have comes from you. I don't ever want to take that for granted. Thank You. Amen.

Build Your House upon the Rock

Build your house upon the rock and not upon the sand.
The house built on the grains of soil will fall and cannot stand.
Storms of life will come and try to pull the building down.
It will vanish in the wind if built upon the ground.
Sands of this world are temporary, yet some fall into dismay.
There are those who hear God's voice and serve Him all the way.
Don't build your soul's foundation on empty, meaningless things.
Build your heart toward the Son and serve Him as your king.
The true rock of God is the word, and His foundation is stable.
He will keep the storms away because He alone is able.

Safe Haven

Be thou my strong habitation, whereunto I may continually resort: thou
hast given commandment to save me for you art my rock and fortress.
—Psalm 71:3

Have you ever felt overwhelmed by circumstances? I would assume that nearly everyone
has known those times. We often face those dark, testing seasons. Outside influences can
bring about frustration and dismal thoughts. God never promised that we would not feel
harsh times, but He did promise to be in the midst of all our trials. We all face difficulties;
nevertheless, we need to remember that God is our refuge. He is our safe haven.

During the 1950s and 1960s, our little coal town of Omar, West Virginia, suffered many
floods. The floods seemed to ravage our area almost every year. Many businesses, houses,
and properties were damaged due to the lack of a local dam. Fortunately, we were one of
the families who happened to live above the waters. We lived on a hill called the 400 Flat,
which overlooked some of the area.

I used to watch some people leave their homes when the floods came, and others would
stay to endure the hardships. I watched neighbors as they swept and mopped the mud out
of their homes and dumped ruined clothing and furniture. When the rains came, they never
knew what to expect. To my amazement, they always came back and fought to keep their
homes.

I admired their determination to stand their ground against the elements.

Watching the people come together was a blessing to me. I liked the way they held each
other up in spite of the floods. I knew some of the people, and they were praying for relief. In
time, their prayers were answered. The government began to invest in the state by digging
deeper creek beds and building dams. Things began to change.

There were better resources to keep the creeks and rivers from spilling over their banks.
Hope began to grow. As I look back, those great people showed true tenacity and strength.

No matter what they faced, they continued to love their homes and families. As a child, I watched the pride of the people stand as one in the face of calamity. The storms may have ravaged the physical properties, but nothing could break their spirit.

It's much like that in our walk with God. We can't foresee the storms that come to destroy our resolve, but we must continue to fight the good fight of faith. We must build and rebuild the things that matter in our lives.

Fighting for the right to live a Godly life is crucial. As we fight, we must trust in God for answers to prayer. The good news is that perseverance and faith do work. We may not suddenly see a drastic result, although God does often move instantly. However, we will see a result in God's time. His time is always right.

Whatever comes in life, we need to remember to run to the heavenly Father. He has the answers we need. You may not see it, but He is behind the scenes working everything out for our good. God is our safe haven, and He is doing damage control for us daily. When the flood of discouragement comes against us, we must trust God in spite of it all. He truly is working everything out for our good.

Moses said unto the people fear ye not stand still and see the salvation of the Lord.
—Exodus 14:13

Shirley's Prayer
Lord, thank you for being patient when I worry over things. You are faithful to rescue me. Help me to never take your love for granted. Place in me a desire to live a pure life before you. I know I may fret, but strengthen me by your power. When life comes hard against me, allow me to trust you through all my difficulties. Establish me in faith through my challenges. I will continue to trust in your ability to rescue me through everything. Thank you. Amen.

Testing Times

Sometimes, life seems unfair and people so unkind.
The more you try, the worse it gets—it's called testing time.
Trials come to test our faith, but hold to hope and love.
It's hard to pass the test without help from above.

Overlook people with vain or prejudiced points of view.
Just hold your head up high, and God will help you through.
Some folks spread dismay, but don't you dare give up.
It's best to never drink the doubts from their bitter cup.

Never let others pull you down with their point of view.
Pray and stand your ground until they measure up to you.
Although we crave acceptance from our fellow man,
Sometimes it's not possible, so we have to take a stand.

Hold on to what is right, and let God correct the wrong.
Our trials come for just a while to teach us to be strong.
When you face a frown and someone's been unkind,
Remember to be patient; it is just your testing time.

God's Help

And straightway the father of the child cried out, and said
with tears, Lord, I believe; help my unbelief.
—Mark 9:24

Jesus was moved with compassion for a father who brought his son to him. The father explained that an evil spirit would often throw the child into the fire and water to try to destroy him. Christ asked the father how long the child had been that way. The father told Him that it had been happening for a long time. The Lord said, "If thou canst believe, all things are possible to him that believeth" (Mark 9:23).

The father loved his son and reached out to the one who was able to heal him. He had reached a point in his life where he knew he could get help only from God. I can only imagine how tender the Jesus's eyes were as He looked down at this young lad. The Lord healed the young child; God is a God of compassion. However, keep in mind that He will sometimes ask us to accept His will for a situation.

Years ago, my mother was stricken with macular degeneration. The disease caused her to go blind. She moved into our home, and we took care of her. It was quite challenging for her when she lost her sight. She needed to learn how to do everything all over again. As a family, we worked with her to help her learn new skills. She needed to be able to maneuver about and find the food on her plate.

Even though she was legally blind, she could still feel, hear, and sense things. She felt the world around her, and the presence of those she loved. Her sight was limited to mere shadows and a hint of the color red.

One year, I decorated the Christmas tree completely in red so she could feel the love we had for her. It was a blessing to see her so very happy. Whatever she wanted, we tried to supply.

When you think about it, isn't that a lot like God? When we can't see things that trouble us, He comes to bless us. God can reach down and touch any situation. He works with us where we are to get us where we need to be.

Our faith, combined with God's love, was enough to get us through. I would have loved to have seen her sight returned, but that was God's decision. Our purpose is to love and support those who are hurting. To do that, we need to let Him help us through our challenges.

In a way, we must become spiritually blind to the temptations in this world to keep our focus on Him. He decorates our days with His best pen. He's the author of our lives and the finisher of our fate. We can stand only as long as we stand in Him. We'll never see all that faces us in this life because God shields us as we go. He carefully prepares each day for us to live and enjoy. Our time is a gift from God. There is nothing that we cannot do with His help. We need to remember that we are complete in Him. Trust God in all things.

"The Lord loves us in our strength and also through our weakness."

Shirley's Prayer

Thank you, Lord, for your all-consuming love. It fills my heart and soul each day. No matter what the circumstances of life, I know your love remains an anchor for me. Please allow me to reflect your wonderful love and light to others. Let those who are in need see that you are the strength of all life. Whatever happens in my life, allow me to remain unshaken. Help me to lead others through your strength in me. Amen.

Seas of Life

When the seas of life are crashing and strong billows sway,
Darkness tries to hide the sun and worry grips the day.
Through these times, God whispers, "Let the storm be still."
My heart can feel the waves subside in obedience to His will.

When turbulence surrounds me or hides sweet heaven's view,
My hungry soul will magnify and dare to make it through.
God's spirit will ascend and bring blessed peace anew,
As He whispers, "Child, don't fear: I am here with you."

Problem Chasers

And Moses said unto the people, fear ye not, stand still, and see the
salvation of the LORD, which he will shew to you to day: for the Egyptians
whom ye have seen today, ye shall see them again no more for ever.
—Exodus 14:13

One day, I watched a little red squirrel run across my yard, over the fence, and upon the top of the garage. My two little Jack Russell terrier mixes ran after him, barking every breath. They saw him run across the fence, but they didn't see him jump up onto the garage.

The squirrel leaned onto the garage top, flipped his tail, and watched the two dogs bark frantically at the fence. The squirrel seemed quite amused at the unknowing, squirrel-chasing dogs who kept barking at him for trespassing on their territory. The squirrel then ran across the top of the garage, leaped into a tree, and got away. Meanwhile, the dogs kept barking at the fence, unaware the squirrel had escaped.

Life is a lot like that story. We get caught up in our problem-chasing and running toward the wrong solutions. We can get stuck on watching a particular situation and lose the area that we need to focus on. We need to let the Lord do the chasing. He knows where the problem started and where it will end.

When we chase the problem, we don't see the real enemy. Satan will amusingly watch us in our frustrations. He works through distractions. His method of winning a battle is to disguise himself. If he can get us to blame someone else or look at the wrong things, he wins. However, God also watches us and waits for us to give up and let Him tackle the situation.

Our Father waits for us to stop chasing problems and realize that we are not endangered by our dilemmas. He has all power and wants to help. The Lord is aware of all our circumstances, and He can thwart off any problems that arrive in our lives. The key is to let Him have the worry and regrets. We can trust Him to know exactly what we need. We must keep our faith in His ability to assist us throughout our journey in this world. When things happen beyond our control, we mustn't try to chase down the answers. Our job is to let Him do His job. He's good at creating worlds and hanging stars to light our path to victory. Don't chase the problem. Rather, rest in the ability of the Lord to know all the answers. He knows what to do even when we don't. God wants us to stop chasing problems that keep our minds weary.

The only way to overcome any situation is to hand it over to the care of the one who created all things. When we chase after the problems, we hinder the answers. The enemy loves to keep us preoccupied with the details. Let God have the situation. He already knows the answer. His delight is in helping His children.

Be not overcome of evil, but overcome evil with good.
—Romans 12:21

Shirley's Prayer
Lord, help me today to trust you with the situations in my life. Fill me with your light and understanding. Free me from heartaches and challenges that propel me to act unwisely. Let me be strong enough to trust you today and always. Thank you. Amen.

Wait upon the Lord

Pondering disappointments of past memories,
Wondering why the hurts came to cause the misery.
Foolish choices made in haste can cause a lot of pain,
But all is well as we trust and call upon His name.
Wait upon the Lord when all ground seems unstable.
There is a rock that is sure, and He alone is able.
He'll take the disappointment and turn it into treasure,
Pressed down and shaken up, blessing come without measure.
Wait upon the answer that God will send your way,
Trust His lead as you go and praise Him all the day.
There is safety and comfort as you walk in one accord,
So be patient as you go and wait upon the Lord.

Trust God

Trust in the Lord with all your heart. And lean not unto thine own understanding, in all thy ways acknowledge him, and he shall direct thy paths, and He will direct your path.
—Proverbs 3:5–6

When I was seven, my brother and I played a game. We wanted to see who could stay longer inside an old trunk that our mother had discarded. Darrell, my brother, got in, and I locked it. He stayed awhile and then knocked to signal that he was ready to get out.

I let him out and then proceeded to get inside the trunk myself. I was determined to out do my brother by staying in it longer than he had. Unfortunately, I stayed so long that my brother got distracted and left me.

After awhile, I got tired of the game and wanted out. I knocked and knocked, but my brother was no where near the old trunk. It was very hot that day, and I was sweating profusely. In the background, I could still hear the music blaring from inside the house. I knew I was in trouble but soon went to sleep.

My rescue came from the arms of a visiting relative. At the time, my brother-in-law, Wilson, had come outside for some fresh air. He thought he heard a kitten inside the trunk and opened it up to find me sleeping. I barely remember him lifting me out of the trunk. Although my brother loved me, he got distracted and forgot me. We spent many years sharing the experience and thanking God for His mercy that day. Wilson is with God today, but I still remember our childish antics, and I miss him.

God remembered me, and He had compassion on a child doing a foolish thing. We were just children playing, but our game almost turned deadly. God saw and mercifully sent the assistance I needed.

My rescue was not a coincidence. It was destiny. God has a purpose for everyone, and He wasn't done with me. That day, I was unable to help myself, but God's mercy rescued me. He knew the next step I needed to take in my journey to Him. Each of us has a journey in this world, and it's God's decision when He will call us home. While were here, we must do His will.

When things try to block our blessings, God will help by providing the escape. He holds the next breath we breathe, and He is the key to unlock the door of our crisis. Sometimes, we make foolish choices that lock us up in what could be called the trunk of despair. Don't worry; He knows where we are and how to rescue us. We must simply wait and trust Him.

"Lift your head; don't feel blue, God loves and cares for you."

Shirley's Prayer

Dear Lord, once again, I ask for your wisdom and guidance through my life. I give you all that I face today. You alone are able to lead and guide me through the ups and downs of my existence. Thank you for all the time you have invested into me by rescuing me from the task of my struggles. I trust you with all my life to lead me to your next step in my journey here. Amen.

Next Step

Lord, help me take the next step down the path of life,
Give me strength to stay the course and do what is right.
Don't let the night that I face subdue my weary soul.
Keep me through your Spirit, and make me fully whole.
Each day is a mystery that only you can see.
You create every moment up ahead for me
Keep me as I go, toward dawn's awaiting day.
Shine your light ahead, and help me walk your way.

Be Not Weary

Be not weary in well doing for in due season ye shall reap if ye faint not.
—Galatians 6:9

Many years ago, when I was very young, I remember complaining to my mother. The protest was about my having to work in the garden and in the kitchen canning at harvest time. I felt disadvantaged and wanted to be with my friends. I realized that when summer came, we had to prepare for the cold and harsh winter months. Yet, as a child, I couldn't grasp it all.

I must have appeared quite selfish as I flaunted my childish ways. I grumbled that all the others kids got to play ball and games outside, and I felt deprived. I wanted her to understand that I was just a child.

My mother was patient as she listened. She seldom allowed me such privilege in my boasting. She was strong and worked hard raising her four children, and I knew that she needed all the help she could get. Yet, as a child, I wanted to run and play likes the other kids. Instead of working in the fields and canning food, I wanted more leisure time.

During one of the coldest January days, my mother asked me, "How does that chili taste?"

It was obvious that I was thoroughly enjoying it by the way I scooped it down. "It's great!" I exclaimed.

She said, "It should be. You helped me can those tomatoes for it. Now aren't you glad you did?"

Her loving words convicted me of my complaining, and I understood what she was saying to me. Yes, I was very thankful for that little bowl of chili that she had prepared. During those cold, intense winter months, those jars of canned fruits and vegetables helped to sustain us. They tasted so good in our times of hardship. We reaped our harvest by the labor of our hands.

While working in God's field, we sometimes get weary. However, one day down the road, the harvest will come in, and we will be rewarded. There is a day of refreshing coming to those who continue to do His will. For now, we are laborers in His vineyard and gleaning in His pasture. While we are here, we should rest in His grace and feast on His Spirit. He will meet our needs, but we must remember that His provision brings responsibility.

"Use me in the harvest, Lord, and help me to believe, though
the burdens heavy, one day I will receive."

Shirley's Prayer
Lord, allow me to trust in your love and appreciate all that you do for me. I'm safe in your hands, and I know you have excellent plans for my life. Nothing can separate me from your love and blessings. Help me to remember that all that I have comes through you. Everything that I hold valuable is your gift to me. Thank you. Amen.

Thankfulness

Lord, I'm truly thankful for all that I receive.
From the bounty of your hand came health and family.
Everything I have has clearly came from you.
In return, I gave you all, what else could I do.

It's not merely words, but I'm thankful from my soul.
Your love has touched my being and made me fully whole.
In return for your love, let me to others sow a seed,
Allow me to help lonely souls, still longing to be free.

Lead me to bring hope to the wounded that need passion
Let others see in me a soul filled with Godly compassion.
I want to share my bread with those who have no meat,
And perhaps I may lead a few to kneel at your dear feet.

I refuse to turn away from those who need a gentle hand.
How could the love of God be reflected to my fellow man?
Keep me on this journey that I may let your light shine through
To show the lost and hurting masses that there is hope in you.

Don't Quit

Therefore, my beloved brethren, be ye steadfast, unmovable, always abounding in the work of the Lord. Forasmuch as ye know that your labour is not in vain in the Lord.
—1 Corinthians 15:58

When the work of our ministry seemed to slow, I would occasionally take a job. During one of those times, I went to work at a nearby hospital. I loved helping people, so I thought the medical field offered me that open door to do so. My schooling taught me to appreciate the wonderfully intricate way God made the human body. While working in ministry and the medical field, I learned that God worked in both areas.

Over the years, I've come across situations I could not understand. There were numerous occasions that brought me to my knees.

Sometimes, I met people with great faith. Years ago, I met a lovely young lady who was about twenty years old. She had been given the worst report a person could get in medical terms—no hope.

My heart melted for her, but I noticed the strength she had in the Lord. Although I didn't know her, I could tell she was a fighter. The doctors had told her that she would not live, but she talked about her faith in God. He had given her His hope. As a Christian, she had a focused spiritual attitude. She had the faith to know that leaving this world was just the beginning of a new life in heaven. She was a blessing to meet.

On the other hand, I've seen some others who have lost all hope in life. Some even tried to end their lives. Some committed suicide because of things that seemed hopeless. The enemy of our soul is relentlessly trying to negate a bad image to us. His job is to make us feel inferior, ugly, or stupid. Think about it! He's the enemy of God; therefore, he's the enemy of all God's creation. God's word tells us the outcome for the evil one. He loses in the end, but he wants to take everyone with him. God came to give His life for us.

It's sad to see anyone give up on life. I don't know why everyone doesn't see the real problem is not in them but in the devil. He paints an illusion that is not real. There is such diversity in people. I've found one very important factor involved. The factor is the God gives hope.

The truth is that only God can give us the hope that brings true peace. Hope is the one thing that everyone needs.

If the medical field could mass produce it in a bottle, this product would heal the world. However, medicine may prolong life, but all hope rests in God. Without God, there can be no hope.

We are housed in a temporary condition called flesh, but we are waiting for a permanent resurrection. Jesus Christ died on the cross to give everyone hope. It's our privilege to cling to its meaning and share our faith with those who don't have it. No matter what we face, God is the answer. He is our only hope. We must stay at rest in the assurance of God's grace.

There is no time for doubtful strife; there's someone watching over my life.

Shirley's Prayer

Thank you, Lord, for today, with all its challenges and tasks. Through them comes my strength and wisdom. You have planned my days—all the days of my life. I know that you care only for my well-being and that you already have the solutions for each trial. I will trust in your love and ability to keep me today and always. Amen.

No Quitting Time

Are you facing a battle and life seems out of rhyme?
Give it all to Jesus; it's not quitting time.

When you go through life's challenges, let your love light shine.
Shine your light for Jesus because it's not quitting time

Do all you can do, and things will turn out fine.
Stand upon the word of God; it's just not quitting time.

Keep your faith as you walk down life's narrow line.
God's assures us by His word; there's never quitting time.

Waiting

*For I will not see you now by the way; but I trust to
tarry a while with you, if the Lord permit.*
—1 Corinthians 16:7

Sometimes, it's hard for us to realize that our God can also control our time with others. Often, we wait in time-sensitive circumstances. The truth of the matter is that waiting can be a stressful matter.

When my son was old enough to work, he decided that he was old enough to stop going to church. He didn't want to go to church because his parents wanted him to attend. I was heartsick over the things he got into as a result of his open desire to explore other avenues.

He left home and moved to California. Our faith was put to an extraordinary test. We loved and missed him, but none of that could break the attitude of alienation. He became distant and unreachable. We couldn't seem to break through the wall that he built up around himself. Through that trial, I came to realize that trusting God with our son's soul was much more difficult than trusting the world with his flesh.

As a child, he was always under our watchful eye and knew that we would do anything possible to protect him. Imagine how shocked we were when he no longer wanted our protection. We knew that he didn't want to hurt us, but he wanted to grow up. He wanted to be allowed to make his own choices and mistakes.

Over the next few years, we never stopped loving him or praying for him. Our prayers were the source of protection that covered him. Even though we missed him, we waited patiently for his return. Finally, he called for help and wanted to come home.

When he called, we were more than willing to help him. Eventually, he came back home to us. That's how God feels about His children. He waits for us to realize that we need His help and guidance. Patiently, He waits, and He loves us even when we make mistakes. Even when we break His heart, He loves us. Sometimes, He will discipline us, but He still loves us.

Remember the prodigal son came to himself and returned home (Luke:11–32). Just like with the prodigal son, our son had come home again. It's good to know that the Lord is like that father. He is more than willing to help us when we call upon Him. No matter how far the distance or what the circumstances may be, He loves us.

God will never leave or forsake us. Sometimes, He says yes; sometimes, He says no; and sometimes, He says to wait. He has a time to answer our prayers. Wait and trust Him. He is always on time.

Though heaven and earth pass away, God's word love will secure my stay.

Shirley's Prayer
Lord, today, I want to thank you for all the wonderful things you do for my life. I realize that there are challenging times and difficult situations ahead, but you are aware of them. I'm confident in your ability to keep me. I am safe within your loving care. Keep my heart fresh on you. I know that you will never leave me, and together, we can overcome all things. Thank you. Amen.

A Son

You are my son, and I want you to know,
I will always love you from the depths of my soul.
You've been such a blessing throughout the passing years.
At times, you've made me laugh, but sometimes, I cried a tear.
I appreciate the little things that you always try to do,
And I realize God's handiwork reflecting out of you.
I've watched you face your battles and overcome some fear,
And I ask God to cover you and hold you very near.
I've often tried to teach you, as mothers always do,
But I've found it reassuring that you have taught me too.
Even when we've disagreed over things we may believe,
With all of my heart, I hasten you to dream and to achieve.
Throughout your life remember, no matter where you are,
I will always love you and believe that you're a shiny star.
You may earn admiration by the things you choose to do,
But love is always in my heart, and that you'll never lose.

Abundant Blessings

Now unto him that is able to do exceeding abundantly above all that
we ask or think, according to the power that worketh in un.
—Ephesians 3:20

Times were hard for most people in the coal-mining towns of West Virginia in the 1950s. Due to the depletion of resources for jobs, most families struggled. We were no exception. One winter, it was freezing cold and had snowed several inches. I walked to school. We lived about a quarter of a mile from Omar Junior High. On one particular morning, I realized I had a rip in my shoe. Not wanting to worry my mother, I put cardboard in the bottom of my shoe, hoping it would keep out the snow.

As I walked through the snow, the cardboard dissipated. My socks were soaked by the time I got to the school. My regular teacher was out sick, so we were placed in various other classes.

My substitute teacher was a sweet lady and known for acts of kindness in the community. I'll call her Mrs. Hope.

I remember sitting in class, rubbing my shoes together. My socks were wet, and my feet aching as they tried to thaw from the bitter walk to school. The teacher must have been aware of my dilemma. She looked at me from across the room and motioned for me to come to her desk. As I stood before her, she asked, "Would you like a new pair of shoes?"

Was she serious? I walked to school in freezing temperatures with holes in my shoes. I smiled and nodded my head.

After a little while, I was taken to the Junior Mercantile Store in Omar. She bought me a pair of little black shoes, and I was elated. I proudly walked home (again in the snow) and happily showed off my new shoes. She was just a substitute teacher for me that day, but she became a permanent fixture in my heart and mind.

I never forgot her kindness. As a child, I wasn't able to help myself. My family struggled to keep heat and food in the house. The wonderful thing about God is that He knew just how to get my needs met. By His design, He sent me to someone who would not only see my need but also sow a seed of love. Out of obedience to God, she acted for Him on my behalf. I'm humbled by the memory but strengthened by the experience. I try to pattern her obedient faith in my own walk with God.

Sometimes we walk through difficult times but the good news is that our heavenly Father walks with us. He works in and through our hardships. His love and mercy is always working ahead of our knowledge of the problem. I never forgot walking through that cold, snowy weather to get to school that day, but I made it. Because I refused to stay at home and quit, God made plans to meet for my need. That's the plan of God. Don't quit on the horizon of your miracle. Let Him fix the problem. Stay the course, and let God control the winds in your sails. We can only put a bandage on the problem, but He can create a new and glorious thing.

He supplies our needs by His love; He'll send down His bounty from Heaven above.

Shirley's Prayer
Dear Lord, this world is subject to your awesome power. Nothing can happen today that you did not allow. Help me to remember that you are still in control of all things and that you're working everything out for my good. I'll rest in your ability to keep, lead, and sustain me. Amen.

Where Can I Go?

Where can I go when life seems unkind?
What shall I do when the sun doesn't shine?
I'll cling to the Lord and hold tight to His hand.
He'll lead me on and make the sun shine again.

Where do I go for all of my earthly needs?
I go to the one who watches all my deeds.
The Father above knows every time I call,
His loving hand supplies the needs of us all.

Where do I go with the questions that I ask?
Sometimes, it's unclear how I must complete a task.
In every situation, I've learned one thing is true,
All answers come from God; He knows what to do.

Living with God

Knowing this, that the trying of your faith worketh patience. But let patience
have her perfect work, that ye may be perfect and entire, wanting nothing.
—James 1:3–4

After school, I would go home to do whatever chore had been assigned for me to do.
Sometimes, I didn't have anything to do, so I would play with my friends. Other times, I had
to help with things around the house. Often, my responsibilities included working outdoors.
Back then, we didn't have the modern equipment to work with. We had a few tools. Our
tools were those passed down by relatives or friends. A few were bought secondhand. We
had a push mower, a hoe, a rake, and an ax to do our outside work. One of the things we
did to supply our home with food was to can it. Since we raised our garden every year, it
was important to prepare for it. Proper care was taken to ensure the health of the plants
as well as our survival. I remember my mother saying, "Nothing can grow out of nothing."

We had to sow the seed to gain a harvest. It's the same way in the Bible teachings. The
Lord Jesus used the parable of the sowed seed to illustrate the importance of a harvest. Just
as we had to prepare our field to receive the seed, Jesus had to prepare our hearts to receive
His word.

I think about the large clumps and stones that we tossed away. We were taught that
they made it difficult for the new plants to grow. A small plant needs fertile, loose soil to
grow and water to nourish it. Stones and clumps only slow plants down and cut their roots
off. Our job was to remove the hindering stones to ensure plant growth.

That's the way God works in us. He expects us to do the work that He left for us to
do. Sometimes, God uses our difficulties to weed the gardens of our own hearts. We often
pick up stones and clumps of bitterness, unforgiveness, and pride. Those things hinder our
spiritual growth. By entering problems and trials, we learn to be patient and forgiving. It's
called Christlike character.

God created us to live and grow strong in His spirit. We are His seed. We are birthed in Christ, but we need the fertile word and spirit to grow. These are the tools He gave us. We must remember to use those instruments for Him in the garden of this world. Our destiny is determined by our faith. Whenever I need to be reminded to keep doing God's work, I remember my mother's words: "Nothing can grow out of nothing."

When the shadows of this world may come, simply,
pray them away and shine like the Son.

Shirley's Prayer
Dear Father, take my heart and use it for your glory. Make me an instrument of your grace. Let me sow love where there is hate, let me sow kindness where there is harshness, let me sow patience where there is no peace, and keep me in your perfect will for my entire life. Thank you. Amen.

Stand

What shall I do when problems come?
I'll watch you, my Lord, roll them asunder.

What can I do when fears block the sun?
I'll hear your voice ring out like the thunder.

When problems come against me, I will trust thy will.
I'll wait for you to lead when wounded, quiet and still.

I cannot calm the ripples in the ocean's stream,
But you can calm the waters and walk upon sunbeams.

Forever I will trust you to be my solid rock.
You always open up the door when you hear me knock.

Love and Compassion

Cast your bread upon the waters: for thou shalt find it after many days.
—Ecclesiastes 11:1

Walking by faith is not always easy. Sometimes, God expects our best to be given to those less fortunate. Early in our ministry, I learned that He will so often ask you to give up that special thing you possess.

Many years ago, in 1978, we traveled to Michigan from our home in West Virginia. I was given a new leather coat and shoes for Christmas by my father. When I opened the gifts he gave me, I was elated. I was so proud of them and couldn't wait to wear them to church. After a few days, we left Michigan and returned to our home.

It was Saturday night, and I wanted to wear my new treasures to Sunday morning church service. The problem came when a teenager and her family came to visited us that night. When she saw the coat, her eyes got big, and a smile came across her face. Then I saw the old garment that she wore, and it melted my heart. I couldn't bear the thought of that young girl not having a better coat. I thought back to when I was a child and others helped me.

I struggled with it at first, but I offered her the coat. She tried it on, and it fit her perfectly. Her face reflected her joy, and she asked me, "Are you sure?"

I was completely sure that I was obeying God.

When she left that day, I thought, "Well, Lord, I'm sowing seed out of my need." I wanted God to be proud of me. It didn't matter what others felt toward me, but it mattered how my heavenly Father felt. Nothing I've ever done for Him has gone unrewarded.

After a few years, I looked in my closet and saw four leather coats. Of course, one was a full-length, black leather given to me by another Christian. His gift to me was a reminder of His approval. God had truly sent me back my blessings. I learned the importance of trusting

God with everything. That happened many times throughout our ministry. Each time, the Lord gave me the same thing or something better than what I gave away.

Sometimes, God will ask for that brand new thing you treasure. He may not ever do it, but if He does, I know He has greater plans. Don't worry; He will always reward the sacrifice. Nothing is more precious than obeying His voice. God is a giver. I've shared this story for forty years, but I'm still drawing from that blessing today. God shared with us Calvary, His Son, and Eternity. He is worthy of our praise. What a gift, and it keeps on giving!

"There is no garment as precious as the garment of praise."

Shirley's Prayer

Lord, thank you for all that you sacrificed for me. Keep your love in my heart and soul. Let me hold to your promises and walk uprightly before all my loved ones and friends. I want to keep a caring heart and loving nature as my sign to the world that you exist in me. Amen.

Love Shines

Don't worry about gray clouds that hide the sun's bright ray.
Although we can't see them, they are there to stay.
Just as many blessings are hidden from our view,
Trust God for added faith, and He will get you through.

The love of God shines in us, and we feel its strong embrace.
We recognize it in the heart and show it on our face.
It is there at all times and with the heart one sees.
There may be cloudy days, but His love shines eternally.

Love's courage is an active view of discipline so intense.
It is the reason heroes act against all common sense.
Love has many faces, but the feeling is the same.
It doesn't hurt or cause reproach, bitterness, or shame.

Hero's Confidence

I can do all things through Christ which strengthens me.
—Philippians 4:19

Work at the church was constantly demanding. There was always a need to plan for a church event, newsletter, bulletin, visitation, or counseling.

One such day in February 2009, I turned my computer on to do some work before our Sunday service. I needed to work on a flyer for an upcoming fundraising event. The computer would not respond to any of my commands. I was instantly frustrated and discouraged.

Because some of my files were not backed up, I thought that I had lost all the important documents. Compounding the situation was that our funds were low, and there seemed to be no way to fix it.

Imagine my surprise when my husband, Tom, decided to fix it himself.

He had never used a computer in his life and knew nothing about them. He did, however, know how to pray and ask for guidance.

He called a few places, talked to some repair men, and went to the local store. After being told exactly how to put more memory into it, he came home and began to work.

I was still reluctant to believe that he could fix the computer. However, since he was so zealous to try, I stood back, watched, and prayed. What could I lose, since it was already broken?

After tinkering with it, he soon said, "Try it again! I think I got it fixed!"

Half-heartedly, I obeyed his excited command. To my amazement, it worked. I had the computer back. Apparently, I must have saved too many things on it. It needed more memory. To be honest, I knew the Lord had intervened.

I gleaned some things from that event. God often teaches us to be thankful for the little things and appreciate what we have. I saw the strong determination in my husband and how much he cared about my problems. I appreciated him even more.

Sometimes, the Lord allows little inconveniences to interrupt our plans to keep our vision right. My husband had the qualifications of a hero to me. He served in the Army in Vietnam during the Tet Offensive, and God brought him home safe. He never stopped being a hero to me.

God gave us heroes throughout the Bible. When we need an example to follow, all we have to do is look at the word of God. We have plenty of heroes there. My definition of a true hero is simple. I believe that there is a hero in everyone, but it needs to come out. True heroes simply do what is right to help others.

"If you feel you have fallen down and lost a battle, don't worry; God will always find you, pick you up, and make you a champion."

Shirley's Prayer

Dear Lord, as I face the world of challenges that life brings my way, allow me to be like you. Let me be an outer reflection of my inner belief in you. When I need to forgiven, allow me to repent. Keep me open to your love and direction of my life. Let me be a shining example of you. Amen.

The Master's Hand

We are just one lump of clay and one grain of sand.
With love, we're being fashioned by the potter's hand.
So gently He prepared us as a little lump of clay.
He mirrored it to shine with His own perfect way.

On the potter's wheel, He shaped us by His heart.
His skillful hand created us with the hope we'd never part.
Our Father holds us close to Him and wipes away our tears,
And He gives us the strength to overcome our fears.

We are God's creation, and He made us through and through.
He knows our strengths and weakness, much more than we do.
Our struggles merely shape us and give us strength to stand.
We are being crafted by our loving master's hand.

Knowing God

Be still and know that I am God: I will be exalted among
the heathen, I will be exalted in the earth.
—Psalm 46:10–11

When my mother passed away in 2006, I adopted her two-year-old dog, a little Jack Russell terrier mix named Baby. She was incredibly loving and smart. Due to the fact that my mother was not able to move around much, Baby watched a lot of television with her.

As a true friend, Baby would lie down and watch the television with my mother. She would instantly jump to her feet and bark when she saw another dog on the television. Baby kept my mother amused by barking at all the doggies on the tube. She was an amazing pet.

Losing my mother was hard, but having her beloved pet made it easier for me. The dog was a little piece of her, and I loved that little pet. She constantly entertained me by her vigilant watching of the television. I amusingly called her my guard dog. I had never seen a dog do that. I laughed at her, and to please me, she began to bark at horses and cattle. She was faithful to me and never let me out of her sight very long. Baby lived to be almost twelve years. As incredible as she was, she could not fight the hand of death.

In this world, we have many precious things to keep us happy. However, this world will not satisfy the living soul. The soul of man yearns for that permanent eternal happiness and love that can only be found through God.

Baby would sound the alarm whenever she saw a dog on television. We need to sound the alarm to let the world know about our God. Our actions are a testimony. What we do is influencing someone in something. It's important to live a Godly life.

People need to know that there is hope in God. He created us to serve our purpose and leave this temporary world. While we are here, our testimony must be one that points to the Lord. We can only reflect Christ's love by example.

Those who live by God's rules will inherit everlasting life. When things hurt us, we find hope in the Lord's promises. His word gives insight into His great love and plans for our eternity. Living for God is a challenge, but that's how God makes champions. Today and always, let your light shine for Him.

"In this life, we can only stand, holding tight to the Savior's hand."

Shirley's Prayer
Lord, thank you for the day you have prepared for me. Allow me to keep my heart and mind in you. Keep me constantly aware of your will and ways as I face life. Help me recognize those things that are needful and do them for you. Direct me as I combat all my fears and conquer all my challenges. I rest in your will. Amen.

The Father's Love

.Snow on the mountain tops and beneath it evergreens,
The waters in the lake below are reflecting heaven's scenes.
Our Lord created everything, as far as the eyes can see.
Revealing His marvelous love to all humanity.

God's glory and unmerited love are reflected in His plans.
He makes provisions for everything by His graceful hands.
This world and all its beauty points to Heaven above.
It's a place where weary souls find rest in the Father's love.

Keeping It Real

But the LORD said unto Samuel, Look not on his countenance, or on the height of
his stature; because I have refused him: for the LORD seeth not as man seeth; for
man looketh on the outward appearance, but the LORD looketh on the heart.
—1 Samuel 16:7

No matter how perfect things look, the truth is that nothing is perfect. Our outlook on
the way things are can be good or bad. The truth is that there are wonderful and beautiful
things all around us. We choose our outlook on them for what they are. We don't always
see the whole picture. I read somewhere that there is a flaw in every diamond. Whether
this is true, I think diamonds are beautiful. I don't buy a diamond for the flaws; I buy it for
the beauty. Life can be what you choose to make of, but we don't always see eye to eye. Our
understandings can be different. For example, we don't always understand our children,
but we always love them.

When my son was very small, he cried for a Tonka truck. He was totally focused on his
desire for the toy. We knew our money was tight, but we finally sacrificed to get him one.

A few days later, when he was outside playing, I heard some loud, crashing sounds
coming from our front porch. When I stepped out the door, I saw he was using a rock to
pound on the new Tonka truck. I could only think about the money that we had spent on
the truck. At that point, I even wished that I had spent it elsewhere.

Frustrated by his actions, I demanded to know what he was doing. Unaware of my
emotional disapproval, he looked up at me matter-of-factly and stated his case. He smiled
at me with his childish grin and said, "I'm making it look real."

I had no words to say to him. We had sacrificed to buy him a brand new truck because it
pleased us to give him our best. I put aside my anger, realizing that he had his own opinions
of what he wanted the truck to look like.

I surrendered my disappointment to his vision of a Tonka truck. After all, it was his truck. Being just a child, he was limited in his perception. He was enjoying the time he spent making it look real.

When I think of that day, I realize how our heavenly Father must feel when we don't live for Him. I'm so thankful that He doesn't judge us by His perfect knowledge. Instead, He helps us in spite of our limited understanding and gives us the opportunity to grow. However, I do wonder what does He think when we want our lives to look real. Sometimes, we put pride and possessions in front of Him. All too often, we try to impress others with our own version of what is good.

What God wants is for us to just live our lives to the fullest through Him. He is always watching over us. If we try to focus our vision of what Jesus Christ is truly like, we should be able to happily follow Him.

Like my son, we sometimes confuse this world with the real things of God. We often try to fit into the world around us, thus causing ourselves a lot of the painful knocks and bruises. However, we are here to give the world the purest impression of Christ. The Lord Jesus came to give heaven's best to everyone who would accept Him. We are enlightened by His word.

The scripture says, "When I was a child, I spake as a child, I understood as a child, I thought as a child: but when I became a man, I put away childish things." (1 Corinthians 13:11)

Our hearts must remain tender toward God, and our spirits must be willing to grow in grace. The world calls many things love, but there is only one perfect love, and it comes from knowing God. It's real and not a fake, watered down version of love. We can inspire the world by being the outer reflection of our heavenly Father. We should reflect His love to the world and keep it completely real.

"Whatever I do, whatever I say, let me reflect God's light each day."

Shirley's Prayer
Heavenly Father, I appreciate you for teaching me what I need to know each day. Allow me to follow you in everything that I do. Keep me from temptation and forgive my childish faults. I'm depending on you to keep me in right standing with you.

You are my real example of perfection. Thank you. Amen.

Eagle's Wings

How graceful the eagle's wings that master the heavenly sky.
They soar aloft earth's treasures and watch as days go by.

There is no sign of struggle in their boisterous, magnificent stride.
They are revelation of beauty in action with articulate versions of pride.

The wind is its creature of riding, mastered by the eagle's vast spread.
There is an appearance of courage revealed from his stately, grand head.

They flaunt a life of sweet glory and are creatures of grace,
Patience is their instructor, and wisdom stern on their face.

Such strength echoes its glory, as masters, of the dominion above.
Soaring aloft in glorious beauty and made by God's magnificent love.

Offering Miracle

But my God shall supply all your need according to His riches in glory by Christ Jesus.
—Philippians 4:19

During the years of our evangelistic ministry, we traveled constantly from one state to another. On one such occasion, we were in Huntington, West Virginia, for a meeting. After services that night, we were exhausted and hurried to get home. At the time, we were about sixty-four miles from our house. It took about an hour to get to our house in Pecks Mill, West Virginia. When we pulled up to the front of our home, my husband realized that he couldn't find the offering envelope.

Since we were desperately trying to come up with that month's rent, we were frantic. Looking inside the car for the money proved to be fruitless. It was no where to be found. We remembered that he had the offering in his hand as he left the church in Huntington and figured he must have lost it afterward. Ultimately, we accepted the fact that the offering was lost. How the envelope got lost was a mystery.

When we got out of the car, I saw the worry in his face. Our bills were all due, and there was little money to pay them. Our whole source of income was through ministry.

Suddenly, we noticed something very surprising. The offering envelope was not missing at all. It was sitting on top of our car. After we got over the shock, we saw that the money was all there. Although we were grateful, it was a mystery.

We rationalized the event, but we couldn't explain it. Could he have laid it on top of the car before we left the church? Yet, even if he had, why was the envelope still there?

After all, we had traveled sixty-four miles around rough, curvy mountain roads to get home. The only thing we could be sure of was that God must have kept it there. It contained a little over a hundred dollars and some coins. We knew that God had supplied our needs. I like to think that His hand lay over it the whole sixty-four miles. Whenever we face battle,

God steps into action. He'll always make a way when there seems to be no way. It's called a miracle.

Refrain not to sow a seed; God's power is ever-present to meet all needs.

Shirley's Prayer
Thank you, Father, for caring for me each day. I'll trust you through all the rough and rocky roads ahead. I know there is no limit to your love and mercy. Help me to demonstrate your attributes to others in all my dealing with them. Don't allow pride or prejudice to taint my image of you. Forgive me when I fall short and teach me to know how to follow in righteous paths. Amen.

When You Pray

Did you wake up today with worries in your heart?
Have you tried to solve problems but don't know where to start?
God wants you to realize that the answers are on the way.
Simply bow your head, bend your knees, and begin to pray.
While you're praying to Him, your Father will give heed.
He will supply all your needs if you will let Him lead.
Nothing is beyond His scope of making all things right:
He'll help when you call, and He will hold you tight.
The loads get much lighter when you give them all away,
God is always standing by to help you when you pray.

Mother's Heart

Seek the LORD, and his strength; seek his face evermore.
—Psalm 105:4

Sometimes, a word of comfort gives the troubled heart the best hope. So often, I've found this to be true. Once, when my mother was ill, I spent a few years watching her. I continued helping and loving her in the face of all the mountains and obstacles she faced.

Even though she was once proud of her strength, the time came when her weakened body needed help. She had gone blind and had heart problems. I was thankful to have her in my life, no matter what.

One day, I walked into her room and found her crying. We had received a barrage of hospital equipment, and she looked so discouraged. It hurt me to see her so upset and worried. I put my arms around her and ask, "Mom, what is the matter?"

She said, "I never wanted to put this on you."

It melted my heart, so I sat down on her bed. I leaned over, hugged her, and kissed her on the cheek. I lovingly reassured her, "Mom, it is my privilege to help. You gave to me all of my life. Now it's my turn. You are my mother, but I'm a great big girl now."

She nodded her head and smiled, "Yes, you are."

Relieved and reassured of her place in my life, she whispered, "I thank you."

At that moment, all she needed was a little compassion. That was the weakest that I ever remember seeing my mother. She had always been so strong. It was difficult to see her body depleting, but I looked forward to each day with her still in my life. That day, my words gave her comfort and hope. My mind flashed back to all the times she shielded me, clothed me, fed me, and cared for my wounds as a child. Those memories gave me comfort and hope to treasure a lifetime. Sometimes, it's the simplest of things done or said that help us.

That's the way our Father works with us. His word gives hope and strength in difficult times. He expects us to do the same to others. A kind word brings hope. Hope shines life into any dark situation.

God will always meet the needs of His children. When disappointments come, we must trust our Heavenly Father to help. He is aware of all our struggles, and His mercy is everlasting.

Therefore did my heart rejoice, and my tongue was glad;
moreover also my flesh shall rest in hope.
—Acts 2:26

Shirley's Prayer

Lord, I'm yours today and always. Keep me in right paths as I struggle to do your bidding today. I know that every path I walk is laid down by your design. As I walk each mile of my life, allow me to please you. Help me to help others by being more like you. Even in my weaknesses, let my faith shine for you. Thank you. Amen.

A Mother's Work

Created in God's image and made from the rib of man,
She is a gentle creature with a tender, outstretched hand.
The heart of what she does revolves around her loves.
She's thankful for the family that God provided from above.
Unselfish in her caring, consistent in her emotion,
She encourages her family with unfailing devotion.
No kindness goes unnoticed by her sweet, tender eyes.
She loves her family most of all, and she considers it her prize.
When problems shadow over and some harm tries to come,
She simply works to make things right, from dawn to setting sun.
Her heart is full of memories that she wouldn't trade for gold,
Of little things her children have done—oh, the stories that she has told.
The universe is not big enough to house the love she bears.
Faithful to those she loves, she ministers constant care.
With choice determination, no job will she shirk,
For nothing can sway a mother from her allotted work.

Full Costume

For verily I say unto you, That whosoever shall say unto this mountain, Be
thou removed, and be thou cast into the sea; and shall not doubt in his heart,
but shall believe that those things which he saith shall come to pass; he shall
have whatsoever he saith. Therefore I say unto you, What things soever ye
desire, when ye pray, believe that ye receive them, and ye shall have them.
—Mark 11:23–24

By Christian standards, we know that faith is being fully persuaded that God can do what
we believe. However, the truth is that we often use the word "faith" without believing.
Have you ever heard, "I know I can," or "If only I believe." Faith isn't words, but rather the
actions behind our beliefs. As adults, we sometimes become encumbered by past and present
experiences that hinder our faith walk with God.

On the contrary, children are open to believing. They can easily believe in mystical or
magical things and transform into their imaginary characters. They can put on outfits and
become whomever they want because their hearts are still tender.

When my son, Tommy, was about five years old, he had a vivid imagination. One day, he
asked me if he could wear his new Superman pajamas outside. "No" I responded, "Because
they are for bedtime."

He looked rather sad and walked away. After awhile, I began to look for Tommy.
Somehow, he got caught up in his fantasy of Superman. He must have forgotten that I told
him that he couldn't wear his Superman pajamas outside. Yet, there he was outside in full
Superman costume.

I had to laugh when I saw him. There he stood, in his brown cowboy boots, (that he
refused to go without), toy gun, and Superman pajamas on top of the chicken house. He was
completely happy and consumed in his little world. As I watched and listened, I saw him
lift up his hand and say, "I'm Superman!"

It blessed me to see him so happy at play. No, I didn't scold him that day for forgetting my instructions, but later on, I reminded him of my instructions. I got my camera that day and took a picture of him instead. He was doing what comes natural for a child. He was having fun.

Sometimes, we are like that with God. As His children, we often fall short of His expectations. However, it is so good to appreciate that our heavenly Father knows our humanity. He never stops remembering that we are His children. We are always growing and needing His guidance. Our lives are supposed to be fully dressed in His Spirit. We are to live by the fruit of His Spirit. Clothing ourselves in the full costume of our God is our armor of protection. As His children, we overcome by believing God is real enough to do what we ask. I'm always reminded of what the Lord told us in His word. "Take heed that ye despise not one of these little ones; for I say unto you, That in heaven their angels do always behold the face of my Father which is in heaven." (Matthew 18:10)

Sometimes, we forget and fall short of His expectations. The good news is that He understands. Our heavenly Father is always ready to love and forgive us as we pray. Often, we must block out the noise of the world to listen for His voice. We must quiet our souls from all the troubles that come to deflect His blessings. He gently speaks to us as His children.

Unlike Superman, He is not a make-believe character but a real God. As our covering, we are blanketed by His power. His love will fill our lives with integrity and righteousness. As we live our lives, we sometimes get caught up in things that aren't exactly right. He softly reminds us to be more like Him. When we are clothed in His Spirit, we reflect His image. I like to think that He forgives us, smiles, and then says, "Look at that ... it's my child!"

Because our ways are not perfect, God's love paved the way by perfect grace.

Shirley's Prayer

Dear Lord, I'm so thankful that you dress me in the garment of praise and allow me keep my life real for you. Remind me to always do things with your help. Don't allow me to form bad thoughts and actions on my journey to you. Forgive my childish ways, and help me keep you the center of my heart. Thank you. Amen.

Quiet, Little Child

Quiet, little child, please listen as I speak.
Take just a moment to sit at the master's feet.
I have plans for you, and I know you must have heard.
It is all written down between the pages of my word.
I wish only the best for you as you live each day.
I will always be right there to show you the way.
I'll be the lamp you need to light the path you trod,
And I'll be the light you need that leads to heaven's sod.
Don't be too busy—relax and just be still,
Take a moment to listen and know my perfect will.

Quiet, little child, don't be so swift to speak.
Listen to humanity's cry for the redemption that it seeks.
My plan was birthed through love, together with my death.
It gives clear path to my throne through the Spirit that I left.
"You can do all things through Christ." This is my perfect will.
When the storms of life may rage, speak boldly, "Peace be still!"
All things are subject to the words I've given you.
Rejoice! Be glad! Live your life; it is my gift to you.
I ask only this one thing—remember my commands.
Seek out the lost and hurting souls, and help your fellow man.

Unshakeable Faith

He that is faithful in that which is least is faithful also in much:
and he that is unjust in the least is unjust also in much.
—Luke 16:10

My husband, Tom, and I were married for forty-eight years. We worked in ministry together for forty-one years of that time. Our love weathered the demands of life's work and unexpected events. We shared a wonderful life, even though some of the days were difficult. I found great strength in his wisdom and practical approach to things. Being a straight shooter, he said what he meant and stood by it 100 percent. His love for God was admirably strong, and he loved life to the utmost.

Although he held the office of bishop in our church, Tom was an avid sportsman. He participated in hunting and fishing and loved watching the games on the television. He had a zeal for life and abundant energy.

When he got sick in November 2012, we assumed it was the flu. However, to our shock and dismay, his symptoms resulted in a diagnosis of stage four lung cancer. We prayed daily for healing and believed in God for a miracle. Over the course of the next two years, I watched my strong, vibrant husband grow weaker and weaker. Watching him endure so many painful tests and chemotherapy was exhausting. Finally, we submitted our faith and accepted God's will.

One day, as he sat in his chair, he looked at me with compassion and said, "Honey, it won't be long now, and I'll be leaving for home. You and Tommy take care of each other."

Then he added, "When I do leave this world, don't let anyone tell you I died. I will never die. I'll live on eternally with the Lord. Absent from this body means I'll be present with the Lord."

There it was, that unwavering faith in God. Tears filled my eyes, but I was assured that his faith was still intact and that his love for God was stronger than ever. He was a champion for the Lord.

A few days later, the Lord called him home. I'll never forget how mightily the presence of the Lord filled his hospital room. The spirit of the Lord came with an intense, reassuring peace that only a great compassionate Father could bring. I prayed as it quietly ushered him into eternity. In this life, the only thing that brings hope is God. It's not what you have, but it's who has you that counts. By knowing Christ Jesus, we have the guarantee of life forever without the penalty of eternal separation from the Lord. When God has us in His hands, He can give us unshakable faith.

"Father, please carry us through and give us strength as we come to you."

Shirley's Prayer
Lord, I'm so glad that you are my strength and song. I'm so thankful for the joy that comes from knowing you each day. Show me how to use the time I have on earth to fulfill your work. You are my protector. Keep your hand upon me today as I walk in your will. I want to please you. Thank you. Amen.

There May Come a Time

There may come a time when my face you will not see.
For when God calls me home, I will have to leave.
My treasures are stored up above and though I know it's true,
I just want to let you know that I will still love you.
There can be no distance in the heart we share,
But when it's time, I must leave until you make it there.
Think of good things, and please try to never grieve,
Knowing you are strong enough helps me to make my leave.
Remember that though you may not see me with these earthly eyes,
In your heart, you'll always know there are no real goodbyes.
The time will come one day for me to go His way.
Yet there will come another day when you will hear me say,
"Welcome home, my loved one; I've waited for you here,
Where love and joy are without measure, and no one sheds a tear."

Wisdom Gained

Beloved, think it not strange concerning the fiery trial which is to
try you, as though some strange thing happened unto you.
—1 Peter 4:12

Every day is a learning experience. The human mind was equipped by God to receive the good and bad from the events of our lives in order to gain knowledge. In turn, knowledge will produce wisdom to help us. For example, a child is born helpless and innocent, but he always learning about the surrounding environment. For instance, is the environment hostile or safe? Sometimes, those experiences can bring about unexpected and unhealthy results.

As adults, we learn to apply the events of our daily lives to help us live better. When bad things happen, we can let them go or hold onto them. The choice is ours.

I heard of a young lady who had been raped, and for years, it altered her train of thought. She was a victim at first but became a victim by choice.

God does not want us to hold onto pains from the past.

I heard my husband preach a sermon many times about the fiery trials. These trials come like fire that burn hard in the soul. The test of fire, however, can bring great victory if we forgive. Throughout the course of our ministry, we have been challenged and often hurt by some very trustworthy people. We learned that the best choice to make is to forgive and go on. The choice is always ours.

When someone is placed in a prison cell and the door is shut, he is forced into that room. However, if the cell is opened, and he chooses to stay inside the cell, it is a voluntary act. We have the right to choose the outcome of any circumstance the enemy uses against us.

God is the key to the door of dark circumstances. Challenges will come, but faith will unlock the door. Jesus is Lord of every circumstance. He will never leave us the victim.

All He wants is our time and faith to line up with His truth. He is the truth that sets all men free. It's not strange to be hurt, but it is unhealthy to hold onto the hurt. God is peace, and He is Love.

Sweet Holy Spirit, make me whole. Sweep over me, and save my soul.

Shirley's Prayer
Dear Lord Jesus, I know that you are aware of everything in my world. You've fashioned my day with blessings and gifts. You have always made a way for me, even in times of hardship. Keep me focused on you today. Don't allow temptations to sway my heart in any form. I'm safe as long as I rest in your grace and mercy. Thank you. Amen.

I Look to You

When I look above the fields of grain, I see the skies so blue.
My soul beholds the beauty and majesty of you.
The hills, trees, and flowers whisper softly above the dew,
"Behold My creation that reflects my heart for you."

Lord, I see your handiwork in every single place,
And when I feel discouraged, I feel your sweet embrace.
You know everything I need, and nothing can alarm,
I love you Lord, and I am sure that I'm safe within your arms.

One day, the love I feel will give birth to rapture's place.
So I'll live in admiration for your wisdom, love, and grace.
No matter what may happen on life's journey through,

My strength will be renewed as I will trust in you.

Unlock the Door

Behold I stand at the door, and knock; if any man hear my voice, and open
the door, I will come in to him, and will sup with him, and he with me.
—Revelation 3:20

One night after one of our revivals, a local man was unable to get into his car. He stood there looking inside his vehicle and seemed very upset. My husband, Tom, walked up to him and asked him what was wrong.

The man grumbled a little and then told him, "I locked my keys inside this car."

The man scratched his head and said, "I need to call someone to come over here and open this door. My wife has keys, but I live about twenty minutes from here."

Feeling sympathy for him, my husband said, "I can take you home if you like and bring you back with the key."

He shook his head, "I've had everything happen this week. Now this! What next?"

My husband patted him on the shoulder and tried to add some humor, "Why don't we pray and let God open the door?"

"What do you mean?" he asked.

My husband replied, "Well, let's pray. I'll stick my key in that door, and we'll see if God can open it."

"That's impossible," said the man said, but he started to smile.

Tom pulled out his key and walked up to the car. "Well, let's try anyway."

To my husband's surprise, the door opened with his own car key. It was a different make, model, and year. By anyone's standards, that key should never have fit the other man's car. We never understood how it worked, but it did. We did see that the man's needs were met. (Afterward, my husband told me that he was just playing around and trying to make the man relax. However, God worked a small miracle for him. God solved the problem.)

So often, we face difficulties that we feel are impossible. We even feel tempted not to ask about things that seem small to us. However, nothing is impossible with God. Jesus is the door to heaven. When doors lock, He opens them. Faith is the key to unlock every door. Some may speculate the incident as coincidental, but we chose to believe it was a divine intervention.

"Nothing is too hard for our saving King, His hand is seen in everything."

Shirley's Prayer

Father God, help me today to bless someone who may be struggling with trials.
Open the door to my heart, and help me to be compassionate and understanding.
Help me strengthen the hand of those who are not able to bear their load.
In everything I do, let me be the light that shows someone that you exist. I
pray that your peace will guide my footsteps today. Thank you. Amen.

Rocky Road

When the road of life gets rocky and the way seems so drear,
Don't allow it to rob your joy or fill your heart with fear.
These trials last mere moments in our earthly time,
They could never anticipate eternal, sweet sunshine.
More excellent is their weight in glory's bounty fare.
Nothing could describe the gems of its beauty rare.
Our mortal eyes can't see just what's ahead in time,
But far more rewards wait, and it is God's gift divine.
When the road of life seems tiresome or rough at its best,
Remember that there's a better day if you'll endure the test.
Our brief conflicts come, and quickly, they will flee,
But God has promised brighter days and a home eternally.
Endure this light affliction until the sun makes its abode,
Don't forget that treasures wait at the end of your rocky road.

Secret Place

Then cometh Jesus with them unto a place called Gethsemane, and
saith unto the disciples, Sit ye here, while I go and pray yonder.
—Matthew 26:36

When I was eight years old, I use to go up in the hills. Like most of the kids back then, I was at home in the hills. There were times that the neighboring kids would gather to play games and explore the territory. There were other times that I would venture off by myself. I would go there to gather blackberries to sell for fifty cents a half gallon. Of course, some of them were canned for use in the winter.

One day, as I was out picking blackberries, I found a little place where silver maple trees grew. It was so mystical there that I felt compelled to linger. I climbed the tallest one and looked out over the landscape. That place became a refuge, especially when things were not peaceful at home. I always felt Gods presence there.

On one occasion, I felt an overwhelming sense of His sweet spirit. Gently rocking back and forth, the earth seemed to engulf His presence. Gods was there, and I could see His hand moving through the trees. I watched the trees as they bowed in obedience to His presence. God came to visit His child. It was amazing.

Shortly afterward, my mother approached the scene. Afraid for my safety, she urged me to stop going there alone. Things were happening in the world that I couldn't understand as a child. Reluctantly, I agreed to obey her.

In the same sense, God is concerned about the safety of His children. He loves us and does not want us alone. Softly, He draws us toward Him and shields us from the dangers of this world. He longs for our fellowship and wants to know what we are going through. His grace will guide and protect us on our journey through this world.

"Lord, keep my heart tender and mild, lead me as a little child."

Shirley's Prayer

Dear Lord, as I start my day with you, please guide my life. Make it pleasing to you. Keep me the apple of your eye, and allow me to take in the anointing of your presence. Patiently wait for me when I struggle with things. Cause me to do those things that make you happy with me. I put all my trust in you. Thank you. Amen.

A Quiet Place

There is a quiet place deep inside my soul.
When disappointments come, it's where I like to go.
This place inside my heart is filled with blessed peace.
There is no room for worry, hurt, or misery.
It's where I talk to God, and He can make me whole.
I go there every time that I need strength inside my soul.
He doesn't mind my tearful eye or my fretful way.
He gently holds me close and wipes my tears away
There is a solemn place, deep inside of me.
It's filled with God's grace and sweet serenity.

Precious Things

Lay not up for yourselves treasures upon earth, where moth, and rust
doth corrupt, and where thieves break through and steal:
—Matthew 6:19

Years ago, I knew a young mother who loved her family. This mother had precious things that were passed down from her own mother. She held them dear to her heart and kept them cleaned and neatly placed upon a shelf. She had a young son about five years old at the time. He was quite taken by the objects that his mother held dear.

One day, as she was cleaning the bedroom, she heard a crash. The sound of glass shattering prompted her to go check on her son. To her dismay, one of the valued knickknacks lay broken on the floor. It had shattered so badly that it couldn't be repaired. The mother scolded her son and wondered why he would do such a bad thing. He started to cry and said, "I sorry, Mommy."

Looking down at her precious child, the mother felt sorry for him. After all, he was just a little boy. There was no way that he would purposely break her treasure.

Getting down on her knees, she pulled him to herself and said, "It's okay. There are plenty of other ones but only one you. I'd rather have you."

The little boy smiled and said, "I will buy you a new one, Mommy."

Smiling at this precious little soul, she realized that he meant the world to her. He was the most valued treasure in her heart.

Reassuringly, she told him, "That will be great."

That was over thirty-five years ago, and that mother was me.

I was young and foolish, but the Lord allowed me to re-examine my priorities that day. I realized the things that I held precious were just temporary. The real treasures I possessed were loved ones given by God. The Lord trusted me with my son, and I did not want to fail Him. Throughout the years, my son has given me countless treasures. He replaced any treasure that he may have broken with love. God wanted me to see the priceless treasure in him.

I've often wondered about many times have we broken God's heart.

Did we disappoint Him through wrong decisions and foolish actions? If we did, it was the wonderful love of God that pulled us back to Him. He brings comfort to the hurting masses. He forgives because He is our Savior. His treasure is in His love. He values us above all else.

As I pass this way, the land of my birth, help me store my
treasures up in heaven and not on earth.

Shirley's Prayer
Dear Lord, help me today to store up my treasures in heaven. As I live, help me to value those precious gifts that are stored inside the heart. These gifts you gave are family and friends. Those are the important things. Don't allow me to put my treasures in earthly attachments. Remind me that my gifts are not the material things. Thank you, gracious Lord. Amen.

Walk within Your Will

Speak to me Lord while I'm quiet and still.
Let me hear your voice and do your perfect will.

Tell me of the missions that you have for me to do.
Help me walk down right paths that will lead to you.

Forbid that I'm too busy to hear you speak my name.
Never allow me to deviate or live my life in vain.

Show me your plans, and help me to fully understand.
Give me courage to face the task and keep your command.

Keep my heart tender, and help me always kneel
To obey your word, keep the faith, and walk within your will.

The Move

For as many as are led by the Spirit of God, they are the sons of God.
—Romans 8:14

We had traveled extensively in evangelistic ministry for over ten years. We ministered in church revivals and did radio at the same time. Our lives were comfortable, and we were happy. We never thought of leaving our home state of West Virginia. Then, one day as I was praying, I heard the voice of God tell me that we were going to move. During that time, I had been trying to find another house in the same area.

When my husband came home, I told him that I felt that the Lord was getting ready to move us. I was not thinking about a move out of state. However, my husband was offered a new church in the same area. The new church would support our ministry and cut our time spent out on the road. Over the next couple of weeks, God began to deal with him about the move and he began to feel the same way.

One day as I was cleaning my kitchen, my mother called. She was telling me that my father got a new home and wanted me to move into his present home. It surprised me, so I said that I would pray about it. Then my mother said, "I'll pay for the moving van and help you get started here."

In her voice, I felt a sense of urgency, and it touched my heart. Was this how God intended to move us? I reassuringly told her that we had to pray about it. Later that day, we prayed, and God confirmed our move to Michigan. We never thought about the direction, but we trusted God. He had already prepared our hearts for the move. We traveled to Michigan in 1988 and started to pastor a church a short time afterward.

For a couple of years, my mother did well, but she slowly began to be more dependent. We moved into a house next door to her to help maintain her independence. It was convenient for both of us during errands, doctor visits, and family time. Through this experience, I learned that sometimes the Lord will direct our path into a completely different direction. We were satisfied with our lives in West Virginia, but God needed our ministry to move.

His will must be our will. Choosing to serve God is voluntary, but obedience is mandatory. The key is to remain pliable, like fine gold, for His use. He knows His plans for us and works ahead to prepare for every journey. We are never alone in our walk with Him. Moving from our former home in West Virginia was not a clear one, but we recognized God's leading and obeyed. We simply trusted the path God chose for us. As His children, we must trust His leading. He knows what is best for us and will move us into His purpose. His move is always in the right direction.

Lord, keep my soul tender and meek, and help me hear you as you speak.

Shirley's Prayer

Father God, I'm your willing vessel today. I ask for your will as I live and work to please you. Keep me safe in your grace. Whatever moves I must make, go before me. Take my will, and make it yours completely. Bathe me in your anointing, and clothe me in your love. I'm aware of my purpose. I'm created by you to honor you in all I do. Make me real for you. Thank you. Amen.

Life Is a Painting

Life is but a work of art the Lord has done in me.
He alone determines what my life will be.
Sometimes he's painted sorrow, while other times it is glee.
It's not for me to question, the life he's painted me.

I'm resolved to live my life with contentment every day,
Because I know His work in me is on constant display.
I'll reflect the very best, so that the world can see
God's unfailing love and care is daily painting me.

I do not know the colors; He brushes in my way,
He alone will choose them, as He paints me every day.
I'm placed inside the canvas of His painting by design;
Until the work is finished in the master artist's time..

The Picture

Let the words of my mouth, and them meditations of my heart, be
acceptable in thy sight, O LORD, my strength, and my redeemer.
—Psalm 19:14

Years ago, a church near our home was doing portraits as a fundraising event. My husband decided to help the church since he needed a new picture for the ministry. He mostly needed it for advertising and business purposes. We told our son that he couldn't go because it was just for his dad. Since our son, Tommy, was used to getting his picture taken, he seemed a little disappointed. However, he didn't make a fuss about it at all.

Finally, the day arrived for my husband, Tom, to go for the appointment.

After he dressed in his best suit, tie, and shoes, he looked both handsome and professional. As he started to walk out the door, Tommy grabbed hold of his pants leg and cried, "Daddy, take me."

For a minute, Tom tried to explain that it was just for his picture and that maybe Tommy could go next time. He hoped that Tommy would be okay with it. Instead, our son proceeded to cry and say, "Please, please, Daddy, I'll be good."

Looking at the clock, Tom realized he was almost late and had to leave the house. Tommy continued to hang onto his dad. Tom looked at me and said, "I guess I'll take him with me."

I reluctantly agreed with him, and the two left for the appointment. When he came home, we had to leave for a meeting and never discussed the issue any further. A short time later, my husband brought the pictures home. When he pulled them out, he smiled at me. He said, "Don't be too mad at me."

When I looked at the pictures, I started to laugh. There sat my husband in his best suit and tie with his son on his lap. Tommy had his jeans, cowboy boots, and a soiled shirt with a rebel flag on it. The striking contrast was humorous. We still have this picture as a sweet memory for us to share.

Tom, who prided himself with his masculinity, could not resist the love of his little boy. He said, "I just couldn't hurt his feelings." Our son's persistence paid off. His motives were simple. He wanted to be in his daddy's lap and in his picture. We should be like that with God. The word instructs us to hunger and thirst after righteousness. He cares about the desires of our heart and wants to picture us in His family.

The path of God is sweet to find, with the gift of love and grace entwined.

Shirley's Prayer
Lord, I need you today as I walk fully in your footsteps. I know that nothing can separate me from your magnificent hands. Let me lean on your wisdom, and guide me to treat others with honesty. I cannot make it through this world without your power. Protect me on my journey. Use me for your glory. Thank you. Amen.

Walk with Me

Walk with me on my journey.
Hold my hand each day.
Let me caress the sunshine
And embrace it all the way.

Walk with me on my journey.
Hold me safe when dark.
Allow this soul to feel your love,
And keep your grace within my heart.

Walk with me on my journey.
Let my soul be blessed evermore.
Allow me to follow my dream
That leads to Heaven's door.

Walk with me on my journey.
Let me bask within your love.
When I follow in your footsteps,
I'll find my home up above.

Good Thoughts

Casting down imaginations, and every high thing that exalteth itself against the knowledge of God, and bringing into captivity every thought to the obedience of Christ.
—2 Corinthians 10:5

One of the things that use to plague me was poor self-image. One year, one of my teachers brought particular attention to my inferiority complex. She handed me one of my test papers and said, "Smile, you didn't do all that bad."

I smiled and said, "I hope not, but sometimes, I feel sort of ignorant."

I was a young adult in school, yet here I was with that same old fear of being inferior. I felt that all my life, and it was still attached to my soul.

The teacher just smiled and said, "You know what? We are all ignorant. It's just that the subjects vary for each of us."

That saying hit home for me. For the first time in my life, I realized that everyone had something that he or she was not excellent at doing. It wasn't that my grades were bad; on the contrary, I had very good grades. It was that my image of me was bad. The teacher didn't stop at telling me about our subject differences, but she added, "I want you to look in the mirror every day and tell yourself that you are special and getting better everyday."

I decided to try her approach. After doing that for a few weeks, I began to believe it. I started changing my negative image into a positive one. The enemy had convinced me that I would fail, and I believed him. God wanted me to see that I was His child and that I needed to trust Him. I began to smile and be that positive person God had meant for me to be. There are things in life that I don't know, but there are other things that I do know.

We are able to overcome our disabilities by hard work and faith in our Father. If we don't speak to the mountains in our lives, they don't have to move. We have to acknowledge the problem and believe in God's creative abilities. He has fashioned us to be special. We are fashioned in His image. He wants us to feel positive and loved. We've got to see that we are wonderfully and marvelously made for the master's use. God does not make junk, and He made everyone of us.

"As I look into the mirror, allow me to see. There's a special person looking back at me."

Shirley's Prayer

Lord, I put my trust in your guidance today. I'm confident in your ability to lead me, even when I don't know the answers. Let me trust in only you and reflect your image at all times. Make me an instrument of your passion and mercy. Let me bring your light into the dark places of someone else's life. If I complain, please forgive me. Teach me your way. Thank you. Amen.

The Mirror

As I look into the mirror, God allows me to see.
There is a special person looking back at me.
Fashioned by His hand with a little touch of love,
I'm created in the image of the Lord above.

He took the time to give me a will to achieve
And to offer my assistance to others in need.
He gave a dab of patience to keep anger in control
To overlook the negative hurt others can bestow.

There's hope in the spirit that God has placed inside.
It helps me to overcome all discouragement and pride.
As I survey the image that goes past my block of clay,
I see the work of God, and He is shaping me each day.

A Few Coins

And no man putteth new wine into old bottles, else the new wine will
burst the bottles, and be spilled, and the bottles shall perish.
—Luke 5:37–39

It was approximately 1957, and I was about eight years old. My older brother, Darrell, and I were playing as we often did by the railroad tracks. We had some neighbors who used to walk the railroad tracks on their way home. A few of them used to drink a lot. One in particular used to hide his bottle by some rocks by the tracks. One day, we watched him, and after he left his bottle, we took it. As a joke, we hid it from him. The next day, he came for it, but he couldn't find it. We sat silently watching and giggled at the scene. I will call him Billy, and he was in his sixties or seventies. He was a kindhearted and a gentle man who never met a stranger.

We knew Billy's wife. She went to church all the time. Her desire was to see Billy saved. Because Billy knew she disapproved of his drinking, he always hid his bottle on the way home. Perhaps it was hardship or just foolishness, but we decided to sell the bottle back to him each time we hid it. This proved quite profitable for a short time. When we gave him his bottle, he gave us some coins. Like most kids, we took the coins and spent them on candy or gum. One day, he came by and told us that he didn't want the bottle anymore. He said, "My wife's been praying for me to get right, so I'm giving this stuff up."

As children, we didn't know what he was talking about, but we knew we had lost our sales. He was smiling when he reached inside his pocket and pulled out a few coins. He handed them to my brother and said, "Now, don't you be doing this to nobody else. I'll be drinking that new wine from now on."

Watching him walk out of sight, I asked, "What's that new wine stuff?"

My brother didn't know either but replied, "It must be better than that liquor."

Later on, we told our mother about it (leaving out our little money deals), and she said it had to do with religion. She had heard that Billy had become right with God. Of course, none of that made sense to us as young kids who never went to church. However, we did like the results of his change. He no longer did the things that displeased God. We watched his life for a few years, and we were saddened by his passing. We were glad that he never came by the railroad tracks to hunt for his bottle anymore. His life was changed. That was over sixty years ago. We never did that again. We were convicted by his change. We were foolish children doing something that wasn't right. We had no idea that God would reveal Himself in the experience. God allowed us to see that prayers can be answered.

God showed us that people do change. When He comes into the heart of a person, He brings a new reason to live. His word inspires us to know that we are a new creation in Christ Jesus.

The great thing is that God is no respect of persons. He can change anyone who wants to commit his heart to Him. Today, we all have the opportunity to drink from that new wine from heaven. It's a fountain that never runs dry. It brings healing, salvation, and comfort and comes new every morning. What a wonderful Savior.

"Glory not in this world of sinful loss, but glory in souls won by the cross."

Shirley's Prayer
Heavenly Father, take my life, and use it today. Help me always lay aside my own selfishness and give freely. Take what I am, and use it for your glory. Make me into your image. Let your light guide me. Give me wisdom to make right choices. Help me to abandon foolish things in the light of you. Thank you. Amen.

My Heart Reflects

As my heart reflects to yesterdays now gone,
I appreciate the memories of my home sweet home.
It remains a special place of treasures to adhere,
With unfolding shadows of my past remaining very clear.

While pondering a simpler time, with loved ones in the sun,
I cling to each moment and embrace them every one.
Sweet reflections in my mind parade those times of year,
Feeling blessed just to know that loved ones were so near.

My soul echoes clearly the bond of each passing year.
The memories of precious times fill my heart with cheer.
As I reminisce about my happy thoughts of long ago,
I feel a warm sensation flushing through my soul.

The Wheelbarrow

And she said, Truth, Lord: yet the dogs eat of the crumbs
which fall from their master' table.
—Matthew 15:27

There was a time in my youth that I adored hats. It was during my grade school years, but I never owned one. During those days, men would come around and collect scraps for their farm animals. One day, a man came by to collected scraps for his hogs. For the sake of this book, I'll call him Rex.

Being the conversationalist that I was at the time, I informed him of my misfortune. He listened patiently to the ramblings of a little six-year-old child. I related to him that I wished that we had money so I could get some hats. He let out a laugh and shook his head. It made me smile. He was a kind man.

Later that day, I learned that Rex was struggling. He had fallen on hard times. He had no close relatives living in the area, and like so many others, he had no job. He made his living the best way he could. He raised a garden and farmed animals.

One day, he showed up at the house with a bag. He said, "Shirley, I got you something that I know you'll love."

When he opened his bag, he said, "I brought you some hats."

There were probably about fifteen different hats in that bag, all fairly used.

It is a very sweet memory. For days afterward, I wore those hats around the house like a Hollywood star. It didn't matter what I had on—I wore a matching hat to enhance the outfit. I even allowed my friends to play dress up in them. Of course, my mother limited my parading around in hats to the house and yard. She told me that I looked great in my baggy shorts and dressy hats. At the time, I thought it was a compliment.

It touched my heart that Rex had given me the hats. I knew we were poor, but he made me feel rich that day. I never realized how he must have felt trying to make his living in a mining town without many jobs. Times were difficult for everyone.

One day, as I watched out the bedroom window, I saw Rex with his wheelbarrow going up slowly by the railroad tracks. He had a full load of scraps. As I watched him, he did something that shocked me. He reached down his hand and picked up something out of the wagon and ate it. It broke my heart to see him that desperate. Even though he had many needs, he took time to bless a child. To me, he had the heart of a prince.

I'm reminded of the prodigal son in the Bible who got so low that he would have gladly eaten the husk that he fed the hogs. Even though he was in desperation, the prodigal son was still the son of a rich man. His inheritance was waiting for him at the end of his journey home. After the trials of this life, there is a day when we will go home to receive a crown of righteousness. It will be given by our heavenly Father, the king of glory.

"Though I may not possess all things, my Father is still the King of Kings."

Shirley's Prayer
Father, I will need your help in everything I do today. You know each mile that I must walk, and you are aware of the trials awaiting my day. In all that I do, please remind me that you know what I must accomplish. In you, dear Lord, I put my faith. Thank you. Amen.

The Time You Gave

I do not want to leave this world
Until I've done my all.
I hope to conquer feats unfurled.
I'll do both great and small.

Before I hear His call to me,
I'll set my mind to rest.
To use the moment on earth wisely,
And spend His time the best.

I purpose not to leave this place
Until His work is finished.
When I stand before the Lord,
I don't want a spot or blemish.

The Piano

Seek and ye shall find, ask and it shall be given, knock and it shall be opened unto you.
—Matthew 7:7

I've always loved music and wanted to learn to play my own. In the mid-1980s, we started a little storefront church near Logan, West Virginia. I always wanted to play the piano, but I didn't know how. One night, the spirit of the Lord moved mightily in our service. Lives were touched and impacted to come to God. It was during that service that I stood up and asked for prayer. I wanted to play the piano, and I wanted a piano to play. I pondered it afterward and wondered if others may have thought it was a selfish prayer. Nevertheless, I felt good doing it at the time.

A few days later, we got a phone call from a nearby music store. My name was drawn from hundreds of others as the winner of a promotion that it had going on. I was to get my choice of piano. It was the answer to the prayer I had given in church. God had answered it quickly and through amazing means. When I went to pick the piano up, the local paper had someone there to take my picture for the news. It was remarkable. Not only had God given me a brand new piano, but He also made sure the whole town knew about it.

After I got my piano from the Lord, I quickly learned the responsibility that went along with my request in church. I got the piano free of charge, but the ability to play would cost me. It cost me time, patience, and increasing prayer. After I began to put my time and effort into the music, I eventually knew enough to play in church. Although I am not a whiz at the piano, I can do my best to bring glory to His name.

Playing the piano seemed like impossibility to me, but God is the God of the impossibility. He is the creator of all things. That night, He created an open door for my anointing, but I had to walk through it. I had to invest in it. Some would say that happened by chance, I respond, "Not a chance!"

Yes, the whole thing seemed remarkable, but it was never an issue of chance because,

I was there the night the Lord touched me. Faith in God moves mountains. The Lord answered my prayer.

The Lord has invested Himself into this world. He paid the supreme price to redeem us from the curse of sin. His heart's desire is to bless His children. In myself, I could see all my handicaps, and I felt unable to play the instrument. God looked past my limitations and gave me strength. When we feel that we can't overcome, God steps in to change all the odds.

"Miracles are just a prayer away, if we can believe Him as we pray."

Shirley's Prayer
Father God, I am so thankful that you know me. I'm blessed that you have placed your presence in my heart and life. As I walk today, please be the foundation beneath my feet and the sky above my head. Let me feel you inside and beside me. Help me to abandon self-will and melt into your image of me. Thank you. Amen.

What Did You Do?

When the time comes for me to leave
This world I'm passing through,
Will He be able to smile at me
When He asks, "What did you do?"

As I stand at the judgment seat,
Will I hear Him say," Well done"?
Will I walk away ashamed
Because I left His work undone?

When my name is called on earth,
I'll stand before His throne.
I hope to hear Him say with pride,
"Welcome to your brand-new home."

The Revival

And he said unto them, Go ye into all the world and preach the gospel to every creature.
—Mark 16:15

In 1976, Tom and I joined church, and shortly after, we began to feel the call to evangelism. We soon moved from Michigan to West Virginia. We were unwise in our decision to catapult ourselves into ministry so fast. It caused us a lot of hardships. We were zealous but not according to knowledge. The good thing was that God protected us and paved the road through every trial. His love and grace strengthened our journey.

We had no open doors at the time, but we believed God had called us. One preacher who knew my husband's father sent a message that we could come to his church to preach. After my husband preached, doors. began to open. We started our first revival in a small church that had very .few members. It was located in Logan Country.

During those days, some churches would leave their doors open. It was a much safer time with a more relaxed atmosphere. Doors were left open for folks to go in and pray during the day. When the revival started, souls began to be saved and healed. It was our first revival, but it left a lasting inspiration on us. It taught us so many things that helped inspire our faith. We came to know some very sweet people who also became our friends.

We had it hard financially, because neither of us worked. Our work was traveling in ministry. We traveled a lot. At the time, the coal mines were not working, and thousands of people were unemployed. Money was scarce, but spirits were high in our revival. In the midst of it all, we soon found ourselves without a place to live. This problem did not stop the revival. In spite of it all, we went to service.

One night, a couple who had been saved in our ministry asked us to their home for dinner. We accepted gladly, and they blessed us so much. We enjoyed our fellowship and ended up staying with them for a number of weeks. We prayed, sang gospel songs, and shared our faith. Their compassion showed the true meaning of Christ's love.

In spite of our rash decision to rush into evangelism, it was a huge learning experience and well worth the sacrifice. The revival lasted six weeks, and sixty-four people gave their hearts to God. At the end of the revival, my husband got news that they were hiring in the coal mines again. Soon, my husband got a job, and we found a place to call home.

Looking back, it could only have been God's hand at work. I've found that in this life, we face circumstances beyond our control, but we must always trust God and remain faithful. As I look back, I can still bask in the memory at seeing God's power at work.

I'm thankful for the journey we took because it gave so many people the chance to know God. It has been over forty-five years since our first revival. I can count my blessing as I see the results of those days. After all that time, I can clearly see the evidence of our sacrifices in God's calling. I'm still in touch with people who committed their lives to Christ through our ministry. Some are pastors, evangelists, and teachers. Others are great Godly anointed musicians and workers for the cause of Christ. What we do matters to others. Everybody deserves to know about God. There are no throw-away people—only candidates for Christ. That first revival changed many lives and impacted many others. Everybody is worth one more prayer.

One day, there will be another revival. It's the one that we will have when we all get together in the kingdom of God. Every saint who ever lived will be there in that holy place. Imagine what a wonderful revival that will be!

"I ask you Lord to be my guide, and keep me safe close by your side."

Shirley's Prayer

Lord, I'm so thankful for your love and patience with me. I ask that you continue to help me to be what you desire. Fill me with so much of your presence that I will never stray from you. Walk with me as I go. Guide me to those who you know need to hear about your goodness and mercy. Thank you. Amen.

Down Life's Highway

Life's is like a highway; take care not to stray.
One must pay attention, and walk the proper way.
When the road is rocky, you'll feel you can't get through.
Trust the Lord to guide; He knows what's ahead for you.

So often we may disappoint and clearly made mistakes.
It's good to know that God is near, and patiently, He waits.
When we realize our wrongs and move toward His love,
He is willing to forgive and sends blessings from above.

He knows it won't take long for us to realize our blunder.
He stands there patiently and thrusts the trials asunder.
Our faults may cause us many days of anguish or dismay,
But He will help to lead us when we take the time to pray.

The Light

Ye are the light of the world. A city that is set on a hill cannot be hid.
—Matthew 5:14

We had been asked to minister at a church near our home. It was a meeting with various music groups, and my husband was to preach afterward. We got to the church about six in the evening and watched the crowd enjoying the service. The little church was packed. However, it was very hot that day, and the only air conditioner was a small wall unit.

Things were going great. The crowd was singing and clapping as it rejoiced in worship. Suddenly, the lights went off and shut it all down. Some of the musicians waited a little while before packing up and leaving. Only one group stayed behind to sing and play the guitar. This group a blessing to the church, even though it was terribly hot.

After waiting half an hour, it was growing dark inside the church. Feeling a little discouraged, the pastor came to the front and announced that my husband was coming to minister. Sweat was pouring off of him.

When my husband walked up to the pulpit to lay his Bible down, he told the people something that surprised me. He smiled and said, "I'm not going to preach in the dark, so we will pray and God will turn on the lights!"

Every head in the building popped up.

"Did he just say that he wasn't preaching in the dark? Isn't that arrogance?" the man next to me inquired.

I looked at him and said, "That's faith, and I believe God can do it."

My husband had everyone stand and begin to pray. For a few minutes, the sound of prayer ushered forth with great enthusiasm. The spirit of the Lord began to move, and God answered our prayers. The whole church lit up, and the air conditioning began to work. Everyone looked around with great joy. God had answered the prayer. The man next to me said, "God did it."

My response was, "I never doubted Him for a moment."

The prayers were answered. Of course, my husband would have preached anyway, but he felt that God wanted to show the people there that day His power. There was a great spiritual renewal that night.

So many times, the enemy comes into our lives to darken our day. The light of God's word always pushes the shadows away. It's faith that ushers in miracles. All God wants is someone to be a light and declare, "I know He can do it!"

"Though shadows come to cover me, God light will cause the dark to flee."

Shirley's Prayer

Dear Lord Jesus, I'm so thankful that you have given so much of you for me. Help me live because of your love and sacrifice. It was you who gave me life, and now I ask that you help me to use my life for you. Wherever you need me, lead me. Guide me to make choices that will bring honor to your life. I need you to lead my way. Thank you. Amen.

The Homecoming Day

My heart sings sweet praise as I go my merry way.
I am looking forward to that great homecoming day.
Down here, I must be patient and do my very best.
I need to walk in paths of love and true righteousness.
The loved ones I hold dear are watching the path I lead,
So I am more determined to walk it faithfully.
I miss those gone before, but they're waiting there for me
In that land where there is crowning love and joy eternally.
There is no night in Heaven, for God Himself will shine,
And the angels will hear us sing, "Amazing Grace" through time.
The walls are precious stones that reflect God's sweet glory.
God's saints walk with angels, professing their kind stories.
I'm on His honored list, and one day, I'll make it home.
It's a privilege to know He chosen me and called me to be His own.
One day, I will graduate from Earth to Heaven's golden shore,
And dine with my heavenly Father and loved ones gone before.
The invitation is still open and all are asked to dine
If you will simply make Him Lord and Father of all time

Break Down

He that dwelleth in the secret place of the most High shall
abide under the shadow of the Almighty.
—Psalm 91:1

After leaving a scheduled revival in Sutton, West Virginia, we were headed home for the night. We planned on returning the next night. On the way home, the highway was very dark. There were no lights. We were hungry and tired and longed to be home. It was nearly ninety miles, about an hour and forty-nine minutes, to the church. Part way home, our little blue Escort suddenly died.

My husband tried to start it to no avail. He got out of the car to wait for a car to come by, but no one came. I could see him pacing back and forth, and I knew that he was praying. There were no cell phones, no stores, or gas stations, but there was prayer.

Inside the car, my son was complaining that he was hungry. I knew that he hadn't eaten since just before the church service, and I felt so sorry for him. I told him that we would have some food in a short while. Telling a child to wait on anything is difficult, especially a six year old who was hungry. I began to pray and reached for the Bible in the dark car. I had a flashlight, and randomly, my eyes focused on the words: "For he shall give his angels charge over thee, to keep thee in all thy ways." (Psalm 91:11)

The words encouraged me in the face of that dark situation. God had given us protection, and He was present. All we had to do was wait on Him. We waited about a half hour. Suddenly, car lights came down the road and pulled up by our car. The man got out and talked to my husband. Soon, they came to get us, and our son out of the cold.

As it turned out, he said that he would normally not be on that road at that time. Apparently, the man had gone to some classes and was headed home. He saw our car and felt compelled to pull over. He stopped to get some equipment and loaded up our car.

Soon, we were on our way home. What looked like a bleak situation became a blessing.

God answered our prayers and took us all the way back home. As God would have it, I learned from that experience. I found that trials come and things can look bleak, but our greatest weapon is prayer. God can rescue His children in any situation and at any time.

God knew exactly where we were. As our Father, He will never leave us nor forsake us in our dark hours of our lives.

No matter where we get stranded in this life, His love will light the way. We need only believe in God's ability to help and allow Him to move in the situations we face. We have to know our worth. God paid a huge price for us. We are the redeemed of the Lord. Our Father values us with all His heart.

From Life to death our lives will span, clutched within our Father's hand.

Shirley's Prayer

Dear God, let the light of your glory light my path today. When the winds of discouragement try to push me back, please be my anchor. Keep the strong storms of disappointment away from me. I will let you shine your will into my soul. I will serve only you as my master. Give me your truth at all times. Thank you. Amen.

Not Alone

You are not alone on your rough and rocky road.
God has you in his hand, and he'll help you bear the load.
He'll hold you close to his heart and always keep you strong.
His love is everlasting, and he will right each wrong.

He can wipe the tears that fall from your weary eyes,
He'll send you gifts of rainbows and bright, sunny skies.
When you feel discouraged, remember not to fear.
You're not alone in the battle; your Father is always near.

The Waymaker

He'll make a way where there seemeth to be no way.

In the 1980s, we attended a state convention in Huntington, West Virginia. We drove approximately two and a half hours and rushed to get to the meeting by seven. We didn't take time to eat a meal but had a snack as we traveled. Attending the event was great. The music was anointed, and the preaching was powerful. There were hundreds of churches represented. It was a very rewarding experience.

We knew a couple of the ministers and went out to dinner after the service. The local restaurants were very busy due to the extra patronage from the event that we had attended. The restaurant we chose was so busy that people were lined up outside the door. Yet, we waited eagerly and talked with our friends as we waited. We stood in line and waited, and the smell of the steak coming from the building made us even hungrier.

Imagine our surprise when we saw two very distinguished men from the meeting walk past the line where we stood. My first thought was that it was rude and made me feel bad. The waitress, not knowing what they did, came and took them in front of us. Not wanting to misjudge the event, we asked the waitress if the two men had reservations. She informed us that there was no reservation. Not willing to make a scene, we held our peace.

After we were sat at our table, we joked about it and dismissed it as just bad manners. We could see them across from us as they gave their orders. Then we waited for the waitress, who soon came to take ours. We had a good time with our friends and enjoyed our food. Afterward, we turned to hear the two people who had pushed their way in front of us complaining. Apparently, they had not received all of their order and were still waiting. We were finished with our meal and headed home.

Sometimes, things happen that make us feel bad. The two men who walked in front of us wanted to be first. They spent no time standing outside in the cold. Yet, they felt they were entitled to go before everyone else. The Lord helped us deal with the issue in a gracious manner. The fact that we forgave them did not keep God from teaching them a lesson in the matter. There are no entitlements in the area of treating others properly. If people would think about the consequences, maybe their choices would be different. We need to always think about how that would make us feel.

Likewise, Jesus made Himself a servant to His disciples. His manner was one that would gladly benefit others. To be an example of Christ, one must remember at all times to esteem others before first. There are no "cuts" to get above or before anyone else.

We live in a world of people who feel entitled to just about everything. The one thing that we are all entitled to is salvation. To gain salvation, we have a God who watches over our lives and expects proper living. We are saved by the Lord to let our light shine in a very dark world. In order to shine for God, we must set the right example.

The Lord made a way for us that night to have a wonderful time in our faith and fellowship. He also allowed us to witness the fact that arrogance and haughty spirits do not always win first place. Instead, He blesses those who choose to live right even when they think no one is watching. He truly is our waymaker.

"Lord, help me to remember that you love every one, and
that you gave us all the gift of you only Son."

Shirley's Prayer
Father God, help me keep my perspectives right. Don't allow me to think
that I'm entitled to everything in life. Keep me tender to your voice. Speak
loudly to my soul, and make me hear those things that are needful for me.
I need you today and always to light my pathway. Thank you. Amen.

Hand of God

Sometimes, we question as we pray.
Remove turbulent waters in our way.
Just know there's nothing God won't do.
He'll keep us safe and see us through.

He gently eases the pain we bear.
He'll hold us close with loving care.
We'll be alright on the path we trod.
Keep holding tight to the hand of God.

Picky Eaters

Therefore if any man be in Christ, he is a new creature: old things
are passed away; behold, all things are become new.
—2 Corinthians 5:17

Living as ministers, we often had very little money. I found it wise to save or freeze most leftover food. I would use it at another date in a different meal. It proved to be a good thing for our budget. We were a family of three, but we all had different palates for food. I would basically eat most things without a problem.

The problem that I encountered was pleasing my husband and son.

My son wanted to eat junk food for every meal; of course, I didn't allow that to happen. My husband, Tom, on the other hand, wanted nothing to do with leftover food. I had to be skillful in my planning of meals. When I froze or saved food, I always put it inside something he loved. I saved pasta sauce or hamburger for chili, vegetables for soups, and fruit for pies and such things. I simply reinvented the meals.

One day, my husband was really complimenting my chili as he devoured his second bowl. I watched with a smile on my face because he had no idea that he was eating leftover spaghetti sauce I had spiced up as chili. Realizing that I had not been shopping, he asked me, "Where did you get the stuff for that chili?"

With complete pleasure, I said, "I reinvented our leftovers. Glad you loved that chili."

It amazed him that he actually could enjoy those leftover foods. He just needed to know that he was wrong in his method of thinking. For years, I tried to get him to eat anything leftover, but he always said, "Not today."

Unfortunately, our budget could not support his stance on food. With that knowledge, I began to do what most women do. I took matters into my own hands and fixed the problem. It was a little deceptive on my part, but when he asked me, I revealed to him what I had been doing. I explained that it cut our grocery bill immensely. He was so pleased to know that

I had been wise in my responsibility as homemaker. Finding out that he actually did enjoy leftover foods was a blessing to him. He just needed to see that he did.

There are so many people who think like this. Often, they judge their likes and dislikes before they even know the full issues. There's an old adage that comes to mind: "Don't knock it until you've tried it."

In a diverse world of responsibilities, we must do what is best for ourselves and our families. The same applies to Biblical standards.

We must learn the scriptures, cultivate them, retain them in our hearts and minds, and use them to help our mission field. Our family and friends are part of that mission field. We have constant contact with them and need to keep the hope of God alive for them. Reinvent new opportunities to engage with them about God, church, and prayer. Most people need to see that you are wise in your walk with God.

Jesus came to earth as God's Son. He reinvented Himself for our sake. He didn't have to do it, but He chose to reveal God through His life and sacrifice here on earth. Many times, we are asked by God, after we come to the knowledge of salvation, to reinvent ourselves. We need to walk a new path, chose new and different friends, become educated with the Bible, and keep communication with other believers. As faith increases, the soul grows stronger. Nothing remains the same after God touches it. When God is in it, things always get better.

"I am as you made me to be, you've given me all that I must be free."

Shirley's Prayer

Heavenly Father, today help me to focus on what you want me to be. Let me remove from me those things that may hinder my faith in you. Keep me free from other's opinions, and give me victory over all my challenges. I stand in faith to remove all my mountains and conquer all my fears. Thank you. Amen.

Cooking

Cooking is my love; I adore those four-course meals.
I fancy adding and subtracting, my flours and corn meals.
I always want to bake, especially if I'm stressed.
The only problem that I have is I have to clean the mess.
The splatters and the splats that I leave on the floor and walls
Don't seem to matter much, until, I have to clean them all.
The sticky pans and utensils are piled high again today,
But cooking is not complete until I've cleared them all away.
Sometimes, the dessert appears like a total flop.
I just change the name, add Cool Whip, and decorate the top.
At times, I forget an ingredient, but it is not my intention.
I simply smile with pride and said, "This is my own invention!"
I try to please my family members because they all think I'm so great.
It thrills my heart to hear them say, "It's the best I ever ate!"
My husband doesn't like leftovers, but I don't throw them away,
I always rearrange the food and send it back his way.
My pintos go in chili, my roast becomes a stew,
Some go into fajitas and casseroles, but he thinks they're all new.
All in all, I'm very happy that God gave me the utmost best.
I'm doing what I love to do in my kitchen-cooking quest.

Father's Arms

The LORD is my shepherd; I shall not want.
—Psalm 23:1

Have you ever noticed that God uses our surroundings to enhance our faith walk with Him? So many times, I've gleaned wisdom and comfort from my life as it pertained to those I love or experiences that I've encountered. Jesus used the same techniques in parables to His disciples as He taught them the scriptures.

He'd say, "There was a certain woman," or "There was a certain man." These were passages that pointed to someone specific. I've found this to be the case with most of us in our attempt to convey our experience in Christ. We've learned by our experience, and that makes our faith more meaningful to others.

I've shared many of my own personal experiences as a means of helping other people. We overcome adversity by our confessions of faith. The word tells us that the redeemed will overcome by the blood of the Lamb and the word of our testimonies (Revelation 12:11).

The Lord wants us to glean from our life and use it resourcefully to gain strength. Many times, others can relate to our testimonies about the love of God. As our heavenly Father, He loves us so much more than anyone else could ever love us. His desire is for us to rest confidently in Him. He wants us to trust Him to keep us safe in all our experiences.

One year, while we were in a meeting in Maryland in the early 1980s, God taught me the depth of His love. It was at that church that I became fully aware of His place as my heavenly Father. He opened up my understanding to how much he loves us. He did so by using a simple but momentous event.

That night, after the service had ended, my husband came back through the church to help me with our son. Our two-year old son, Tommy, lay fast asleep on the pew next to me. I watched as my husband gently pulled him up to himself. Our son's opened his eyes just for a second and recognized that it was his daddy's arms helping him up. He gently surrendered to his arms and peacefully went back to sleep. I observed him as he snuggled his head on his dad's shoulder in full trust that he was safe and that his father would get him safely home.

Isn't that the way the Lord is to us? In this chaotic world, we can become exhausted in our physical journey. Our flesh may want to bow beneath the heavy load of discouragements. However, in the essence of faith, we must rely on God's strength to pick us up and carry us through. We need to always think about how much our heavenly Father does to gently and safely guide us to Him. He is always nearby to help His children. Sometimes, when we become weary or feel that we can't make it through, He stands ready to come to our assistance. Although we are human, He delights in being there to help us in our hours of need. Like my son, we need to surrender ourselves to our heavenly Father's arms to carry us.

As the good shepherd, He comes to rescue His Lambs. I read once that in times past, when a shepherd would find a wounded or hurting lamb, he would pick it up and carry it to safety back home. He would tend the wound and nurture the lamb back to health. That's how the Lord is to His children.

When He sees His children wounded or hurting, He comes with open arms to help. He'll carry us through the darkest nights and bring back the joy that He intended for us to have. There is joy in the knowledge that our Father is always watching over us because His loved us.

The word says, "The next day John seeth Jesus coming unto him, and saith, Behold the Lamb of God, which taketh away the sin of the world." (John 1:29)

As our shepherd, He will pick us up and lay our head on His shoulders. He will carry us onward to victory. It is good to know that we are always safe in our heavenly Father's arms.

We are wrapped in the arms of God, and He lightens up the path we trod.

Shirley's Prayer
Lord, I'm yours to use at your bidding. In all areas of my life, please clean my thoughts, purify my heart, and renew my spirit. Always make me see the good side of those things that the enemy uses to cause me pain. Let me glean something positive out of all my trials. Thank you. Amen.

Carry Me

Carry me when I am weak and when darkness passes by.
All my hopes reside in you, my comfort and my guide.
When stormy trials compass me and cause my soul to fear,
Help me, hold me, keep me safe, and stay forever near.
Although I know my trials come, only for my good,
I simply ask forgiveness if I have misunderstood.
This mortal flesh cannot see the fullness of your way,
So please forgive its lack and help me through today.
I promise to listen carefully as I hear you speak.
Lord, I ask one thing of you, carry me when I am weak.

Childish Views

When I was a child, I spake as a child, I thought as a child; but
when I became a man, I put away childish things.
—1 Corinthians 13:11

Looking back throughout my life, I can think of so many things that I've had to learn through the process of time. We all gain knowledge the same way. Life is one great big lesson. I like to think about good memories; I find encouragement in them. As God's children, we are gleaning in life's field of possibilities. Sometimes, as parents, we look at our children with proud, adoring smiles. I wonder if we often make our heavenly Father smile with the little things we do.

As a mother, I still smile over things that my son did many years ago. Although I've learned that wisdom comes from many pathways, I know that our greatest source of wisdom comes from the Bible and applying its principles to our daily life. We gain knowledge from life's experiences, and it makes us wise to a certain point. We store that knowledge and apply it throughout life. We learn from bad experiences to avoid negative situations, but good things prompt fondness and hope. Good memories are precious and a constant source of joy.

One of my favorite memories is of my son when he was only four years old. When I think of that special memory, it brings me joy. It happened years ago, when we lived in a house near a pond full of fish. A few beautiful white ducks lived by that pond and swam there daily. One day, we took him over to the pond so he could use his new fishing rod and possibly catch a fish.

I sat by the pond to read a book that I had brought with me as my husband and Tommy fished. After a few minutes, Tommy came over and asked me about the ducks. He wanted to know where little ducks come from. I told him they came from the eggs. I tried to explain quickly that ducks hatch from the little eggs around the pond. I could see he didn't totally understand the answer, but he went back to his fishing. After a bit, I turned to see Tommy trying to dust off the back of his pants.

I walked over to him and saw that he had sat down on a couple of the eggs and crushed them. He had broken egg shell fragments all over his trousers. I tried not to embarrass him as I smiled and asked what he had done.

He looked so sad, realizing that he broke the eggs hurt him. In fact, he thought he was helping the little, white duck hatch her eggs.

As a parent, I thought about how often I tried to do something that turned out wrong. At the time, I didn't understand the full ramifications of my actions. Often, we can make mistakes by not seeing the clear picture. In doing so, we learn from our actions. Time is a great teacher.

I had not taken the time needed to explain about the little duck eggs, and my son improvised with his own solution. Later on, he came to realize the greatest miracle was in letting God perform His magic on the little eggs. Eventually, the ducks hatched and without Tommy's assistance.

Too often, we try to help God do His work for Him, but in doing so, we hinder the process. God is patient and allows us to learn from our mistakes. Sometimes, the process is painful, but it has a purpose. Behind the purpose and the pain is God's plan. He's our Father, and He our best teacher.

Teach me, Lord, each passing day, so I won't do things my own way.

Shirley's Prayer
Dear Lord, help me today to think as you would have me to think. Keep me secure in your will. When I don't understand things, please reveal to me their meaning and give the answers to all my questions. I'm safe as long as you lead me. Though I make mistakes, please forgive me. Always help me consider others as I react to events that reflect on you. Keep my love alive for you. Thank you. Amen.

Tommy's Hatching Ducks

Tommy loved the ducks that swam daily in his pond.
Every day, he watched them, and each day, he grew more fond.
He liked the way they shined so white against the water's glare.
He thought about how nice it was in knowing they were there.
One day' he asked his mother, "Where do baby ducks come from?"
She said, "God will help as they're birthed in the sweet, warm sun."
This puzzled little Tommy, who loved the ducks so dear.
He watched the little goose one day who laid her eggs so near.
When the goose walked away and left the eggs alone,
Tommy went to help the goose, and the eggs he sat upon.
The eggs crushed beneath him, and that made Tommy cry.
"I wanted the little ducks to live, and I made them die."
He wept, "I don't think I can hatch those little eggs,
And I promise not to try again—it will be my pledge."
"Oh my child," the mother said, "Some eggs do not hatch at all.
Only those special ones bring baby ducks and they are very small.
Don't worry now; the ducks don't need you now,
They can have their little ones because only they know how."
Patiently, he waited for the goose to lay her eggs again.
"I know she is about to hatch the eggs, but I can't say when?"
"You needn't fret about goose eggs," He heard his mother say.
"She knows just how to protect them until that special day."
So Tommy waited patiently for the duck eggs to appear,
And then one day, he shouted, "I think the goslings are here!"

He heard the goose quacking loudly in the breaking of the dawn,
And she brought the parade of five proudly down the lawn.
"They're beautiful," Tommy smiled, "I love them every one."
"I'm glad at last I know just where baby ducks do come from."

To Tommy. Thanks for the memory. Love, Mom.

Whosoever

For God so loved the world, that he gave his only begotten son. that
whosoever believeth in him should not perish, but have everlasting life.
—John 3:16

Have you ever wondered where it was that you heard about the Lord? I mean who was that one that told you about Him. We can all share our stories about the evidence of God in our lives. Each experience will be different, but we all learn from someone the meaning of salvation. In the late 1950s, I was in the second grade. At that time, I was probably seven or eight years old. It was during the January months that I became sick and was taken to Logan General Hospital in Logan, West Virginia. I was hospitalized with stomach pain that had kept me up all night. At the hospital, I was one of several people placed in a section called the sun room.

One day, an elderly country preacher came to visit his wife who was in the bed next to mine. During his visit, he walked over to my bed, introduced himself, and asked me very gently, "Do you know Jesus?"

I wasn't sure what he was asking me at the time, but I felt sure that I wasn't aware of what he meant. My reply was simply, "No."

He asked me if I believed that God gave his son. He explained to me the events of Christ dying for every person in the world. It intrigued me to hear his message. He told me about the passage in the Bible that gave credence to his philosophy about believing in Jesus Christ. Then he explained John 3:16 carefully and stressed that everyone would fit the qualifications of a sinner. He said, "Whosoever believed in Him should not perish but have salvation."

He took time to explain what was fascinating to me as a child. I was a bit curious and asked, "Am I that whosoever?"

He smiled and said, "Why, yes you are, my dear."

That precious man of God reached down his hand, bowed his head, prayed for me, and led me in the sinner's prayer. His words seemed like magic to me. He said, "Now you need to read your Bible."

I smiled and agreed that I would read the bible. I have to admit that at that point in my early life, I couldn't understand much of what I needed to read.

I knew that it was important to read, so I would try. I planned on doing my best to do as the old preacher advised.

Later that day, he left to run an errand. Before he left, he spoke with his wife for a moment, and with her approval, they decided to give me a gift. When he came back, he walked over to present me with their gift. While he was out doing errands, he bought me a very popular coloring book for that era of time. He also gave me a little red purse. I was very happy with the gifts from that nice couple. The gifts to me showed their kind heart toward a sick, little girl. After a few days, I went home. God had touched me in my physical body but also in my soul.

I like to draw from that memory when I feel down or discouraged. God sent me a blessing and the word to encourage me during a very dark time in my life. Many hardships came my way after that time, but I always found hope in knowing that I was a whosoever and that God loved me.

God's love is unconditional. It doesn't matter how you live or what you did in life—all God requires is changed heart and faith in Him. God just wants each of us to know that we are a whosoever." He gave His life to give us eternal life. We are special because He made us unique. No one is the same, but we are all loved the same. He wants only one thing of us, and that is our total love. Salvation is not gender-, race-, or age-specific.

Grace covers all sin, disease, or temptation. By accepting His grace, we are blanketed by the His spirit. The message I received that day has never failed to help me. His words gave life and light. I finally had opened eyes to God's love and acceptance of me. That day, I found that God brings hope in all our hopeless situations through love and prayer.

> He came not into the world to condemn the world; but
> that the world though Him might be saved.
> —John 3:17

Shirley's Prayer

Father God, I'm here in your presence, asking for your blessing. Help me to work only with pure heart and clean hands as I deal with others. My heart is yours to direct. Remind me when I forget to thank you for all my blessings, my family, and my friends. Help me remain strong in you. Thank you. Amen.

Before I Can See You

Before I can see you, Lord, my heart has learned to know.
I can't see you with my eyes but only through my soul.
For in this life, we live and do long to be set free,
Until at last freedoms crown brings perfected liberty.

Before I can see you, Lord, I must close my earthly eyes.
I must avoid hate of bitterness and foolish compromise.
I need not gaze on things that pull my soul from you.
I'll try to shield my eyes and think of love and truth.

Before I can see you, Lord, I must lay aside all fear.
I shun blindness in my heart when others shed a tear.
Compassion can come only from those who learn to love,
True love comes as a gift from the good Lord above.

Before I can see you Lord, my heart must be pure.
My soul must brush aside the trials that I may endure.
When I've looked beyond what mere mortals can see,
I will recognize at last, your grace has set me free.

Glimpse of Heaven

In my Father's house are many mansions; if it were not so, I would have told you.
I go to prepare a place for you. And if I go and prepare a place for you, I will come
again, and receive you unto myself; that were I am, there ye may be also.
—John 14:2–3

Knowing CPR was a requirement for the registered nursing degree I studied for in college. I reluctantly took the course but hoped that I would never use it. Near the end of my education, I had to withdraw from my classes due to my mother's illness and dependence on me. It broke my heart, but I've learned to prioritize things, and family is extremely precious. I have never regretted my decision.

Although I pondered the use of my CPR training, I've learned that being prepared is the best solution in approaching any problem. I was working in the medical field during this process of my training and enjoyed it immensely. While working, I came into many situations that required immediate action. Training kicks in when you are provoked suddenly.

On one occasion, I was faced with an emergency involving an accident of a teenage girl. Arriving at the scene, I examined her and found her completely unconscious with no visible pulse. I immediately started CPR. All the while, I was praying for God's intervention as we waited for the paramedics to arrive. Her precious family faced a crisis that only God could solve. Hearts were broken, and tears flowed, but prayer was prevalent. After a few minutes, I checked and thought I felt a slight pulse. It gave me hope as I continued to work with her even after becoming weak myself. I knew that I must continue to work and fight to keep her helpless, little frame alive. Every breath was hope to her and for me.

At some point, the paramedics came and took over for me. One of them told me that he thought there was a slight pulse. I was relieved that he could confirm my suspicions. It gave me hope for her life. However, it broke my heart to see that young teenager so helpless. I watched as the paramedics pulled away and continued to work with her. I continued to pray for a miracle. That precious young teen was powerless to defend herself, but God knew where she was all the time. Later on, I found out that her life was spared. After a lengthy hospital stay, and by God's amazing grace, she lived. She went from hopeless to hopeful.

During that critical episode, I realized how much God fights for our every breath on this earth. He is constantly hearing the knocks on His heart to intervene into our daily dilemmas. His heart is tender toward us as His children, and He keeps struggling to breathe hope into our lives. Sometimes, we get knocked down or have sudden problems that try to paralyze our faith, but God's love is always present to assist us. He breathes His Spirit into our infirmities and heals our diseases. His power covers all trials, pain, and sorrow. All we have to do is be faithful and call upon His name for strength in our dark situations. In this world, countless lives struggle to overcome, and some of them are touched by our faith. Isn't it extremely important that we have something eternal to offer them?

I struggled to help and did all I knew to do for that teenager, but God was the one who gave the healing needed. As so many times before, I saw God's power move into a critical situation. We all need the breath of life that comes from the Lord. That sweet Holy Spirit still comes to refresh and preserve His people. In the book of Genesis, we read about how God breathed the breath of life into Adam. God's breath is still giving life today.

Thinking back, I recall how I was reluctant to learn the medical procedure that helped in saving lives. Today, I can thank God that I did. Being prepared for trouble is the best solution to any problem. Just as I was prepared to do the CPR, I must prepare my soul for overcoming all my trials. Through faith and by reading God's word, prayer, and praise, I'm prepared to work for Him. I can keep my soul prepared for sudden enemy attacks. We must be strong in the Lord and the power of His might. All hope rests in God and faith in His ability to meet our needs when we call.

I will walk this lonely road leading to my crown, forsaking
all to follow Christ where all my hope is found.

Shirley's Prayer
Dear Lord, as I come to you today, I ask for your strength and guidance.
You are my peace amid all my struggles. Give me your blessing to continue
to grow in you. Don't allow things or circumstances to sway me from your
path. Help me be godly. Keep me real for you. Thank you. Amen.

My Glimpse of Heaven

I dreamed of a city, such sights to behold.
I saw the walls of jasper and the street of purest gold.
The tree of life was blooming where no sin could ever be.
I had a glimpse of heaven and the great eternity.

The son, He shined so bright there, like a diamond in the sky.
There were no more heartaches or tears to dim the eye.
All things were made perfect—no more pain or misery.
I had a glimpse of heaven and the price he paid for me.

I had a glimpse of heaven of the street of purest gold.
I saw my friends and loved ones and riches untold.
I stood beside the crystal sea, and the Lord stood with me
In my glimpse of heaven and the home that waits for me.

Amazing Grace

And he said unto me, My grace is sufficient for thee: for my strength
is made perfect in weakness. Most gladly therefore will I rather glory
in my infirmities, that the power of Christ may rest upon me.
—1 Corinthians 12:9

I used to love to hear my father play his harmonica. He would sit for hours, lost in the music. His answer to problems resulted in his slipping away to play. One of his favorites and the one that he played up to the night before his passing away was the song "Amazing Grace." The old song is not just a pretty one. It is also a song about redemption. The man who wrote the words was John Newton. He was a former slave trader who ultimately repented and gave his heart to Christ.

That song has been played for well over two centuries and listed in several novels such as *Uncle Tom's Cabin*.

That beautiful song is sang and played at many funerals and churches. It is a transmitter of the thought of God's greatest gift. We have that amazing grace that came from God through His Son. Christ made a clear path through the demonic forces of the spirit world that tried to stop the will of God. He made a path of righteousness for His children to follow.

One night, while we were in Ohio, I was singing this song, and a man stood up and declared that God healed. As the music lowered, He went on to testify that it was not the single most important gift that God gave him. Although he thanked God for his healing, He clearly gave God the glory for saving his soul from eternal damnation. His face was full of joy as he wept and glorified God. That man touched my heart with his faith. He was well aware of his physical healing but valued his soul above all else.

Through time, I was fortunate to see many healing and souls saved. Through it all, I realized the great importance of God's gift to us. I came to value that amazing grace the song represented. It tells the story of our hope, God's plan for mercy.

It doesn't matter what the enemy does. He cannot stop God's children from loving and serving the Lord. He will help His children prosper in even the worst economic times. He is Lord of our lives and loves us eternally.

Grace is still amazing, some two thousand years after the gift of life that Christ gave to humanity. The songs of grace are songs of love, hope, and redemption. Christ is still giving His grace to those who will receive it. He still saves, heals, and delivers His children. From the heart of a former slave trader came the reflective mercy of God. Now and forever, grace is truly amazing.

There are no unimportant people in the family of God.
By loving others, we pave our road leading to heaven's sod.

Shirley's Prayer

Dear Father in heaven, today I ask for you to reveal to me all your will in every situation. I know that nothing can erase your love and grace. Let me reflect those things to others who come close to me today. I need your healing for all my cares. I need your direction for all my problems. Instill in me your way. Thank you. Amen.

Grace

When I grow weary from life's pace,
I know I can rest in God's amazing grace.
His hand will hold me in tender peace.
He makes the shadows of discord release.
The helm of life leads each day,
But His grace ushers the storms away.
Oh, the price of His great will
Both humbles and satisfies me still.
Nothing can flaw His master plan.
He paid the cost for redemptive man.
As time surrenders to His grace,
My soul shall glory in His sweet face.
When I grow tired, I shall yet glee,
For the grace of God has covered me.

Protected

He that dwelleth in the secret place of the most High shall abide
under the shadow of the Almighty. I will say of the LORD, Hi is
my refuge and my fortress; my God; in him will I trust.
—Psalm 91:1–2

I grew up in small coal town where everyone knew his neighbor. The house where we lived was an old coal company house owned by the mines in our town of Omar. All the houses were nearly identical. These two-story houses could often be used to house two families. Sometimes, they were shared as apartments, with one apartment on the top level and one on the bottom level. Both had three rooms and were joined by a common stairway at the exit. All were painted the same colors, mostly green or yellow. Most were fueled by coal fireplaces and heaters. Our home was rugged with wooden floors that my mother always put linoleum rugs over. Every wall was papered to keep the heat inside.

One night, when I was ten years old, I was awakened by pounding at our front door. Looking at the clock, I saw it was three in the morning.

The person outside was banging on the door and yelling quite loudly, but I couldn't understand him. I got up, ran to the door, and stopped short of opening it when my mother yelled out, "Don't open that door!"

My mother was a tough mountain woman who didn't mind putting anyone in his place. I looked to see her with her gun in hand. By this time, I could hear the man shouting profanity. He seemed quite agitated.

When the door opened, the stranger continued his tirade. He continued to yell at her. By this time, my mother yelled out, "I can smell that liquor all over you. I don't want no drunk banging on my door at three in the morning. My kids have to go to school in the morning!"

The stranger laughed and continued to threaten her. As a child, I knew that he was in trouble and had gotten on the rough side of my mother. As he continued to shout, my mother lifted her pistol from behind her and pointed it at his face. I heard a loud bang when she pulled the trigger. The shot whizzed by his head, and I heard a yell as he scattered off the front porch. I stepped outside to see her shoot again as the intoxicated man jumped down the side of the hill into a briar patch. I could hear him yelling as the briars tore his flesh. My mother calmed my fears at the whole fiasco, turning to me and saying, "Now don't worry, that varmint will never come here again. Then she smiled and winked. "I'll be ready for him if he does."

I'll never forget that night because I saw the strength of my mother, who stood ready to overcome anything to protect her family. She was the strong one who stood between her children and the enemy. Fortunately, things turned out great, but she was willing to do whatever it took to defend our home. That's the way the Lord is with us.

God doesn't have to use a gun, but He uses His Holy Spirit. He protects us from an enemy called Lucifer, who tries to break into our hearts and minds each day.

The enemy loves to catch us off guard, like the night the stranger visited our home at three in the morning. The good thing is that God never is caught off guard. He is always watching over His children. His eyes are open, and His ears are listening for us. His angels encamp around us to protect us from everything. When the enemy comes in like a flood, the spirit of the Lord will lift up that standard against him. We stand complete in His power. He is our great protector.

Thou shalt not be afraid for the terror by night; nor for the arrow that flieth by day.
—Psalm 91:6

Shirley's Prayer
Lord, I trust you today. Keep me in the right paths that lead to you. If things get too difficult, please lighten the load or give me strength to bear it. Protect me as I deal with all the circumstances. Nothing is more important than your will.

Struggles

Sometimes, we face distress and struggle with concern.
Situations often press, and there seems nowhere to turn.
We can cast all cares on God; He knows just what to do.
He will lead each footstep and light the path for you.

When our lives are shaken, and weeping endures the night,
Remember joy will come again with the morning's light.
Life may take a wayward turn and cause our hearts to fear.
We must trust God's sweet grace and know that He is near.

Great Big Fat Hen

Then he took the five loaves and the two fishes, and looking up to heaven, he
blessed them, and brake, and gave to the disciples to set before the multitude.
—Luke 9:16

Have you ever had things impact your life with such a positive influence that you wanted
to pass the blessing onward forever? I've thought about a couple of things that impacted my
life. There is one event that I'd like to share today. I call it my great-big-fat-hen Thanksgiving.

As memory serves, it was a simply act of kindness to my family during a Thanksgiving
holiday, but it made a lasting impression on me. I've shared this story countless times
because it helped me learn a valued lesson about giving.

It was a cold day in November in Omar, West Virginia. We were a week away from
Thanksgiving and had no plans for festivities. Our food was essentially what we had always
eaten. We had beans and potatoes, canned foods, flour, and cornmeal. Although we were
very thankful for everything in our lives, there was no formal dinner planned for us that
holiday. I remember it being somewhat discouraging; however, reasoning kicked in and
reminded me of one of my mother's favorite expressions: "There are people all over the world
with a lot less to eat."

On that cold, snowy November evening, a knock came at the door. I ran to open it door
and found three ladies standing outside. The group made its apologies for showing up
unannounced but added, "We are from the local church and have some groceries for you for
your Thanksgiving dinner. We hope it is alright."

I smiled as I watched the strangers bring in several bags of groceries. One of them made
another apology by saying, "We don't have a turkey, but we have a great big fat hen for you.
We brought all the trimmings with it."

This act of generosity touched my heart. I remember thinking that I wanted to do that
someday.

Even though I was a child, I asked the Lord to let me help others in the same way we were helped that holiday. It was the sweetest feeling to think that someone would try to help us, even though we never attended a church. My life was touched so much by that instance that it carried over into my present life.

Every year around Thanksgiving, I'm reminded of the love and compassion of those people and their charitable act. God showed up just in time for us on Thanksgiving. That was a jubilee year for us, and I've never forgotten it. It was amazing.

Time passed, and my husband, Tom, and I started pasturing a church in Redford, Michigan. I was so pleased to be able to help others during the holidays. For the past thirty years, God has allowed me the privilege to do so. Our church has given out countless of baskets with turkeys and all the trimmings. We can't feed the world, but we can do our part. It is always such a great blessing to help men, women, and children during that time of year.

It's the little things that stay with you. It was a little act of kindness that sparked my life. I've always cherished that day. You may ask, "Do I feel that God placed that in my heart?"

My answer will always be, "Yes, I do."

It was a long time ago, but it lives in my heart today. The church gave us a hen, but it was the seed that brought forth a harvest for the past thirty years. Every year, we've fed those less fortunate. I've found that God uses our everyday life to teach us His way. He was our greatest example in giving. He gave His all to all of us. Love should always be on display, even when you think no one is looking, because someone is watching. His name is Jesus.

Beloved, let us love one another: for love is of God; and every
one that loveth is born of God, and knoweth God.
—1 John 4:7

Shirley Prayer
Precious Lord, once again, I come to you in need of your presence. Heal me from all past wounds and help me to be more like you. Lead me in paths of righteousness, and allow me to always demonstrate true love. Let me lead by example in all that I do so others can see you living big in me. I am your yielded vessel. Thank you. Amen.

My Heart

My heart is yours, sweet Father divine.
You came to rescue this soul of mine.
I was lost, and you made me whole,
You gave the passion that burns within my soul.
The surge of love springs deep within.
My soul longs passionately to keep you in.
Without hesitation, I have chosen to dare
And rest completely in your loving care.
You give my life such joy and thrill.
I love you now and always will.

Printed in the United States
By Bookmasters